Heaven Help Us

Short Stories Volume Two

by

Dale Roy Erickson

ACKNOWLEDGMENTS

To the only true God and His Son, Jesus, who brings us grace, forgiveness and life; Connie Erickson who has stood with me through all of life's adventures; Danney Clark for his significant contribution to this effort; Larry Patrick for his friendship, insight, encouragement and creative graphics design; the Prayerful Publishing board of directors for their prayers, wisdom and support; Kelly Roberts for her gracious and painstaking editing; and to the host of people who challenged us to keep pressing on to the finish line. It's not over yet and the best is yet to come.

Preface

The short stories of Heaven Help Us Volume Two can each stand alone and should be appreciated by anyone. They are part of a multi-platform curriculum designed to help young people grow in their connection with God. The short stories volumes one and two are designed to be part of the homework for the curriculum. The 35-lesson curriculum will include 35 short stories, a smartphone application that provides seven thoughts on prayer with the supporting Scripture for each lesson (a total of 245 prompts), an active participation student manual, a teacher's manual with guidelines for teaching the lessons, a session planning sheet for each lesson, additional teacher resources, and of course, tests for each unit.

The curriculum is designed for the following possible settings: release time courses for public schools, middle school and high school youth groups, home school, Christian schools, and the training of indigenous Christian leaders.

Table of Contents

Searching For Paradise I

She knew deep down that what she was feeling was not rational, maybe
not even real. The familiarity of the streets, the smell of the air, even the
friendly greetings of passersby on the street stifled her as if a weight
were crushing the air from her lungs. She wanted, she needed to be
somewhere unfamiliar, anywhere but here. She longed for change. Her
moodiness and short temper had not gone unnoticed by her family and
close friends, but no one knew the battle being waged inside her mind.
Gradually the feeling overwhelmed her and it no longer mattered if it
was irrational. She knew she must get away. The closer she came to
graduation and her eighteenth birthday, the less she could endure her
mundane existence, and the more desperate her hope of leaving it all
behind.

The things that used to matter were now unimportant and seemed
to have no part in her future. Even family, religion, and her boyfriend
held little interest as she continued to feel inexplicably drawn to a life of
freedom and adventure. Once she had arrived at her destination, she
would tell them she was safe.

Rachel knew she was from a great family. Her conversations

with friends made her very well aware of the fact she had it better than most. She didn't know a single classmate who didn't have some issue in their family life. Her long, auburn hair and beautiful, hazel eyes made her popular with her classmates. The word around school was that she was not only "really hot," but also smart enough to put you in your place. She had no time for fools and could quickly make one look foolish. Deep inside, in a place that no one knew, she had already begun her new adventure. She had it all, but could already see the life laid out for her. And, in her view, it was boring. How could her friends settle for such a dreary lifestyle? If her parents knew the plans she had prepared, they would blow a "disappointment gasket." No heated conversations; simply a myriad of questions followed by a look of bewilderment in their eyes.

There was no time now to deal with the emotional fallout of her plans. She had to prepare for prom, final exams. And then there was Curtis. They had been dating for a couple of years, and he was the envy of every guy in town. Not only did he have Rachel on his arm but he was also the best athlete in the area. To make it worse, he was genuinely likable. His great sense of humor and natural charm made him hard to hate-even if you hated the fact that he had everything you wanted. Somehow after the prom she needed to find a way to let him down easy. It's not like she intended to hurt him. Somehow she had let that issue get away from her. They were good together. Everyone knew that they were meant for one another and would someday get married, have children, and live the good life in Wilder, Idaho. Little did they know the real dreams she held in her heart, a heart bursting at the seams awaiting her quest for excitement and meaning.

~ ~

"Where is your head today?" Curtis asked, interrupting her dream fest. "We are supposed to be studying. I've got to ace this test. Come on, you know I need your help."

"Sorry, where were we?" she asked.

"Where were you is a better question? I'm trying to nail this calculus test, and you're not helping."

"You know, Curtis, my purpose in life isn't built around making sure that you pass calculus," she said with a touch of sarcasm. She knew that it was unfair to push back at him, but figured this might be a good time to start preparing him for the inevitable.

Curtis looked a little hurt and confused. "Listen, if you're not going to help, could you just give me a little space so that I can get something done?"

This presented the perfect opportunity for Rachel to make her exit. "I'm just not up to studying today. Maybe we can take another run at it tomorrow."

As she got up from her chair and headed for the door, Curtis said, "Let's make this work. I really need to do well on this test."

"Tomorrow then," Rachel said.

Curtis mumbled, "OK."

~ ~

She had little cash and less experience concerning travel and what might be required of her in her new venture. She had saved the cash that friends and relatives had given as birthday gifts, and secretly dipped into the funds her parents had put away to help with her first year at the community college. She felt like she was stealing, and yet she could not help herself. It's not like the pittance they had put in there was going to take her very far. Besides the community college was their dream for her. But not the dream she wanted to pursue.

Studying for her exams should have been a snap. She was a good student and picked up on things quite easily. But this year her study times always seemed to drift away to a distant shore. It would start with a stroll on the beach taking in the warmth of the sun and the joy of total freedom. There were no deadlines, no responsibilities, and most of all no one with great expectations. Her daydream would start with selecting the bare necessities. She knew that for this to work she would need to pack everything she needed into one backpack. Trips to Cabela's in the "big city" of Boise provided her with some seed thought for how she might make this happen. She would need a lightweight backpack with comfortable shoulder straps, a lightweight sleeping bag, and a rollup foam pad. She was smart enough to know she would need really comfortable shoes, some flip-flops for the beach, socks, underwear, a good hat, pepper spray, and a Leatherman tool with an LED light. *Oh, forget the flip-flops*, she thought. *I'm going barefoot on the beach.* Most of what she would need on a day-to-day basis could be picked up when she arrived. For now she had chosen her favorite pair of jeans, which she might cut off into shorts, and a couple of tank tops. She took the college fund money and purchased a one-way ticket to Honolulu. After she found a job, her first purchase would be a bathing suit suitable for paradise. Her parents would definitely not approve of her choice.

~ ~

Prom night was everything a young couple could have wanted. The streamers decorated the gym in purple, gold and white. The DJ did an exceptional job of selecting a great mix of songs. Everyone was dressed to perfection. Curtis looked handsome in his rented tuxedo, and Rachel's parents had spared no expense to help her look her best. She was all dolled up in a formal gown, up do for her hair, manicured nails, special makeup, new shoes – the works – and it was working. The chaperones kept an appropriate distance, and the chatter around the tables made for a night to remember. Romantic expectations ran high as new couples fumbled their way through first dates, and established couples had thoughts of taking their relationships to new levels. Rachel did a masterful job of hiding her inner feelings. This was not the night to let Curtis in on her changing view of their future together. She wouldn't take this memory away from him…at least not tonight. She felt sorry for him. The truth was that she really liked him and cared about him. He had a lot invested in their relationship, but that didn't mean she was ready for the future he wanted for their lives. How could she walk the tightrope of not ruining his prom night and reigning in his expectations?

After the dance, Curtis broached the idea of heading out to the bonfire. A group of couples had set aside a batch of firewood at a location that was undisclosed to the parents and chaperones. It was a "Wilder night" tradition to select a location out of the sight of prying eyes and make prom night complete. Everyone knew it was going to happen, even the parents. But the young people knew enough to keep the right people in the loop and certain ones out of the loop. When the kids came home to change into more comfortable clothes most parents gave a concerned look as they told their sons and daughters to "be careful out there." This gave Rachel her opportunity to step off the tight rope. In front of her parents she said that a bunch of the kids were going out to Rodeo Lane for a bonfire. Curtis knew immediately that Rachel's parents would never approve of the alcohol, drugs and other elements of that setting.

Rachel's dad seized the opportunity to raise his concerns. "Rachel, you know that we talked about this. Your mom and I have high expectations for both of you."

Rachel's mom jumped on the bandwagon. "Isn't there some other place where the two of you could get something to eat and still have a good time?"

Curtis knew of her family's commitment to the Christian faith and wanted to have a future with Rachel.

"I'm sure that we could take a drive into Boise and find a nice place to get something to eat," he suggested.

"Hey, you kids have a good time, but don't stay out too late. Your mom and I both have to work in the morning, and you know we won't get a lick of sleep until you guys are back home safe and sound," Jake said.

Rachel was looking for this exact opening. "Thanks, Mom and Dad, we'll try. But this is prom night, you know."

When they got back in the car, Rachel took control of the "bonfire" conversation she knew was about to take place. "You know they are going to ask us where we went. My mom will probably even ask me what we had to eat."

6

Curtis' look of disappointment was all that needed to be said. Rachel had dodged the bullet and would work hard the rest of the night to make the conversation light and pleasant despite the guilt she was feeling. She wasn't being fair to him in all of this, and she resolved right then and there to prepare him for the day she would let her real feelings be known.

~ ~

Curtis' birthday fell one week before graduation. His parents surprised him with a birthday/graduation gift of a motorcycle. It wasn't brand new but had a pristine look. Deep inside Curtis was a little disappointed. He was tired of driving his beat up old car and had hopes that he might get a new one for graduation. His parents could afford it. It's not that he didn't want a motorcycle. He had already shown enough interest to take the STAR rider training course. It was an expensive but valuable course, and it showed his parents that his interest in cycling was real. It didn't take long to get over his disappointment. As soon as he

 took the crotch rocket for a spin he knew that he could wait a few months to get an upgrade on his car. This summer he was going to have a blast on his Honda and save a boatload of money on gas. His first stop with his graduation gift was at Rachel's house.

She wasn't nearly as impressed with his machine as he was.

7

"You don't actually expect me to get on that thing?" she complained.

"Come on, Rachel, live a little. You are always talking about how you want a little more adventure in your life," Curtis urged.

"Actually, I would like to live a little. But it doesn't look to me like this thing will bring me back alive. There isn't even a real seat for me. You want me to sit on that?" she said, pointing to the tiny seat just above of the tailpipe.

Finally after a lot of urging, Curtis got her to throw her leg over the back fender and climb on.

"Hang on tight," he said, as he dropped it in gear, popped the clutch, and fired it down the street. Of course, she had to hold on tight, as there was no other option. As first she hated it, but as she got used to the pull of going through the gears, she actually understood the appeal of riding. The acceleration had a thrill of its own. She found she enjoyed wrapping her arms around Curtis while they blazed their way through the curves. Her mind went back in time to many other moments when she had wrapped her arms around him. *Good times ... good memories.*

That is your past, Rachel, not your future, she thought. *Get a hold of yourself. Don't get lost in the momen*t. *We really have had a lot of fun together. Maybe she could make a life here with him.*

~ ~

There were final exams to get through and then all the special events lined up for graduation week. Rachel's mind was overwhelmed with the conflicting thoughts of what she was hiding from everyone in Wilder verses her dream of simply flying off to paradise. *Why does it have to be an either/or situation? I need to talk this out with someone I can trust. It would have to be clandestine. If my parents got wind of what I am planning before there is no way to stop it, they would be furious and I would lose the chance to just slip away. Brook ... Brook could be trusted.*

Rachel and Brook had shared secrets many times before, and Brook had proven herself. Rachel gave her a call and set up a meeting at the Moxie Java coffee shop in the nearby town of Homedale. That would be far enough away to avoid being overheard by the small-town gossips. When they arrived, Rachel chose an out of the way spot where they could talk freely.

Brook opened the conversation. "OK, what's so important that you made me drive all the way to Homedale?"

"I've got something to tell you, and this one is for your ears only. Agreed?" Rachel asked.

"Of course," Brook said.

Rachel's mixture of guilt and excitement burst out like an erupting volcano. "On the day after graduation, I'm flying off to Hawaii."

"Wow! Good for you! How did you manage that? Is it a graduation gift?" Brook queried.

"Sort of. I've saved up a little money and expect to get some money for graduation. I bought a cheap one-way ticket that leaves on Sunday."

"One way? Why would you do that? Is Curtis going too?" Brook asked, in a flurry of questions.

"No. I'm going alone."

"What? What does Curtis have to say about your plans?"

"I haven't told him yet. I haven't told anyone about this until just now. I'm feeling a little guilty about that, but I'm stoked about the idea of living the adventure."

The conversation went on and on about how Rachel had been feeling trapped in the little town and how she wanted to get a taste of what life could really be like. She revealed her inner conflict of wanting to get away and yet knew it would break Curtis' and her parents' hearts. Brook asked a lot of questions about how she might make it all work out, and tried to get her to put it off until she had given it more thought. But Rachel had made up her mind.

"Rachel, have you prayed about this?"

Rachel had an answer but, chose to just look away. She then got up from her chair. *Prayed about it?* Rachel thought, as they went to pay the bill. *I thought Brook knew me better than that. That kind of religious nonsense is exactly what I am trying to escape.*

Both left the coffee shop with a lot of questions and concerns.

~ ~

Graduation day was a blur. It included all the expected speeches about how important this milestone was and the incredible future they could all pursue. Rachel's mind was filled with all the counter arguments: *not in this little town, the best most of us could hope for is being a rich potato farmer or marrying one.* Curtis had his mind set on getting a job at the Simplot plant down the road. He knew one of the supervisors and there had been a subtle promise of finding a place for him. Rachel applied every analogy in the "hope for the future" speeches to her plans for the next day. Every other thought during the graduation ceremony was on how she was going to break the news to her parents and Curtis. She had gone over the conversation a hundred times in her head, but now that it was truly upon her it had a very different feel. *I'll wait until after the family graduation party and break it to them just before bedtime.* This is the day she longed for and dreaded. *Keep your focus girl. You'll get through this, and they'll get over it*, she tried to convince herself. She couldn't get up the nerve to tell Curtis. He would be crushed and confused. Rachel justified her decision by telling herself that in the end he would be better off. *Did he really want to get married to someone who would always be waiting for and wanting more out of life?*

When she finally broke the news to her parents, they were dismayed. The conversation with her parents ended with Rachel saying, "I'm 18 now, and the truth is there's not a thing you can do to stop me." She then turned, walked into her room, and shut the door.

~ ~

Jake and Marie sat at the kitchen table shell-shocked. There were no words that could truly express the despair they were feeling. Thoughts of how they might have failed as parents were fired into their minds by Satan. Their hearts were full of questions of how they could have missed seeing this coming.

"You know, we have to call Curtis. She can't just fly off to Hawaii without saying a word to him," Marie said.

"She will be furious with us if we do that," Jake replied. "Can we risk sending her off in that way?"

~ ~

"How could she do this to me?" Curtis said, as he stepped through the door of the Martin household.

"If we knew the answer to that she would probably be staying. We don't know any more about this than you do," Jake said.

"I don't know what I did wrong," Curtis complained.

"We know how you feel. I don't think you've done anything wrong," Marie said. "At least that's what she told us."

"Where is she? I want to talk to her."

"She's in her room, but she doesn't know that we called you. She's not expecting you," Jake said.

"Well, she's not getting off that easy," Curtis said, going over to knock on her door.

"I already told you that I've made up my mind and there's nothing you can do about it," Rachel shouted through the door.

"Would you just open up the door and let me talk to you?" Curtis said.

What's he doing here? Rachel wondered. *How in the world did he know about this? Brook, did you betray me? No, she wouldn't do that. It must have been Mom. What am I going to do?* "Just give me a minute, all right? I'm not dressed. Give me a chance to get out of bed." It wasn't true, of course, but she needed a minute to collect her thoughts. "What are you doing here?"

"What am I doing here? What am I doing here!!?? What in the world is going on? You're flying off to Hawaii tomorrow, and you didn't even think I had a right to know?" he shouted through the closed door.

"I just thought it would be better this way - for you, I mean. I was hoping to avoid this whole stupid conversation. We don't have a future together. I'm not going to spend my life in this one-horse town. I have a life to live, and I'm about to get it started," Rachel said defiantly as she opened the door.

"I thought we had a life, a future, together. Does everything we've shared mean nothing to you?" Curtis asked with deep disappointment in his voice.

"Curtis, you are awesome. You mean more to me than you know, and I couldn't have hoped for a better friend. But ..."

"But what?" Curtis asked, cutting her off in midsentence.

"But I can't see us having a future together. I know I would always be searching for something more."

"Something more than me?" Curtis protested.

"Don't take this personally. It's not about you."

"Clearly it's not about me. It's all about you, and I'm just some baggage thrown under the bus."

"It's not like that. This is why I wanted to avoid this whole conversation. *This is getting us nowhere*, she thought. "I have feelings for you, but I've just got to go out and find myself. I have to explore this world and pursue my dreams."

"And I'm not part of your dreams? I thought we had something special."

"We do. We did, but it's over. I'm leaving for Hawaii in the morning, and who knows where after that. You need to know that we don't have a future. The sooner you understand that the better."

"I know you well enough to know that I'm not going to change your mind tonight, but you'll regret this and I'll be here waiting for you," Curtis said, defiantly.

"I need to get some sleep. I have to be up early, and it's a long flight."

"Can I at least take you to the airport?"

"No, I've already taken care of everything," Rachel said, as she led him out of the room and shut the door. *I knew there was no point in talking to him. One day he'll understand*, she told herself as she broke out in tears and cast herself on the bed.

~ ~

It was a sleepless night filled with excitement and regret. Morning finally arrived, but not soon enough for Rachel. She was so glad her flight left at nine o'clock. In spite of her misgivings, Brook had agreed to take her the airport, and true to form she arrived at the house at six a.m. As Rachel quietly slipped out of the house, her parents got on their knees and asked Jesus to watch over her. It was quiet at the house and a quiet ride to the airport. The wait inside the terminal seemed to last forever. Rachel asked Brook to head back home. Brook reluctantly agreed, but made Rachel promise to give her a call when she arrived in Hawaii. During the flight Rachel made a determined effort to fill her mind with the adventures ahead rather than the mess she was leaving behind.

14

~ ~

As Rachel got off the plane and entered the terminal, a Hawaiian greeter said, "Aloha e komo mai."

Yes! Let the adventure begin! She already knew she was in paradise because the airport had an open-air mall that displayed flowers more striking than any she had ever seen. The beautiful colors and unbelievable scents of the flowers captivated her senses. She knew them all from her dreams and research on the Internet. She checked them off one at a time: white and lavender orchids; reddish-orange heliconia; pink plumeria; purple and gold dewdrops; and of course the Hawaiian state flower, the brilliant yellow hibiscus. It was a balmy eighty-five degrees, and she was immediately struck by softness of the humid air. It was a far cry from the arid climate of southern Idaho. After her trip past the tropical garden her next thought was, *I can't wait to get to the beach!* The second thing to flash into her mind was, *Oh crap, I need to buy a bathing suit. Oh well, my cut-off jeans will just have to do for now. I'll hit the ladies restroom and change as soon as I get my backpack from baggage claim.*

After changing her clothes, Rachel asked an airport employee where she could catch a ride to Waikiki Beach.

"There are several options," he replied. "The cabs are right over there, and will run you about forty-five dollars. The courtesy shuttles for the hotels are over there, and they are free if you have a reservation, and about twenty dollars if you don't. You can take the OPT bus if time isn't a concern. That will only cost you two fifty."

"Mahalo!" Rachel said, and headed over the Oahu Public Transportation staging area. *Waikiki here I come!* As she stood waiting for the bus, she scanned the area. She stood motionless, trying to take it all in. Of course, there were palm trees everywhere, each with a little different shape and hue.

When she boarded the bus, she asked the person sitting next to her if she could buy a beach towel near Waikiki. She was told that most of the shops in the hotel area sold beach towels, but the street vendors would probably be less expensive. Rachel opted for a street vendor and was also able to get some suntan lotion.

The beach was packed with people. There were families with children, couples holding hands, and muscular guys everywhere. Of course, her new adventure would have to include some romance. This would be no secluded getaway. This was going to be living life to the hilt, with no limits, no questions, and no looking back. She covered herself with suntan lotion, picked out a nice spot, and started soaking up the rays. *Now this is heaven!* She had seen Diamond Head time and time again in television shots, but seeing it in person was an entirely different thing. It was time to jump into her new life, and it would start with a swim in the Pacific Ocean. She was shocked at the warmth of the water. Several years before her parents had taken her to the Oregon coast. Despite their warnings, she just had to take a swim in the Pacific. She thought she was going to freeze before she got back to shore and wrapped herself in a blanket. This was entirely different. She felt like she could stay in the water all day.

When she finally left the water and went back to the beach she realized how little preparation she had put into this day. She should have gotten a bathing suit when she bought the towel. Her normal clothes were wet and filled with sand, which wasn't going to work out very well for the rest of the day. Traveling with just one backpack left some serious limitations in the clothing area. She suddenly realized she didn't know where she would sleep. She couldn't afford two hundred dollars a night for a Waikiki hotel room. She knew there were beach patrol officers, so she couldn't sleep on the beach. Solving this issue would have to wait until after she tried the Great Hawaiian Hot Dog stand. She was too hungry to think about tonight's accommodations.

It had already been a full and wonderful day, but night was approaching. Then an idea popped into her head. She had seen a sign at the air terminal listing rental cars that were available for eight dollars a day. She could take the OPT bus back to the terminal and rent a car. She would not only have a place to stay tonight, but wheels for a trip around the island tomorrow. This was a great plan. When she arrived at the rental car courtesy counter she smiled and said, "I'd like to rent one of the eight dollar a day cars."

"Sure, can I see your driver's license?" the agent asked. "Oh, I see that you are only eighteen. We can only rent cars to people who are twenty-one or over. Are your parents with you?"

"No!" she said indignantly. "I really need a car. Isn't there something you can do?"

"Sorry. How about a friend? Are you with any friends that are twenty-one or over?"

"No, I'm traveling alone."

"Really, why would you do that? That's no way to really enjoy the island."

"Can you get me a car or not?" she asked with her frustration beginning to show.

"Sorry, we can't help you." He looked past her and said, "Next."

Wow, she thought, *no one treated me like that in Idaho. I thought this was supposed to be paradise. I guess he didn't get the memo. It's time to deal with the problem at hand. Where am I going to sleep tonight? I've seen people sleeping at the airports when their flights are delayed. Maybe I'll just pick out a good spot and spend the night here. I'll deal with finding something better tomorrow.* She found an out of the way place not far from a Starbucks and settled in for the night. An airport security guard came by as she was making herself comfortable. She explained that she was hoping to catch an early flight. He wished her luck and moved along.

The next morning, Rachel awoke with a very sore neck. The beach towel she used for a pillow wasn't exactly the best solution, but *c'est la vie. Today's going to be another beautiful day in paradise.* She decided to catch breakfast at the food court. Her budget allowed for a sausage and cheese croissant, hash browns and an orange juice. It was clear that the first order of the day would be finding a place to work. Her graduation gifts were generous, but she could see that paradise was going to be expensive. She fired off a quick prayer asking God for help, though she was unsure how it would be received. *Why would He help me find a job when I left Him entirely out of the decision-making process up to this point?* A Scripture verse rolled through her head, *"Trust me in your times of trouble, and I will rescue you, and you will give me glory."* *Where did that come from?* She wondered. *Well, I sure hope its right.*

She spent the morning looking for jobs at the many hotels near Waikiki. Surely they would have a lot of turnover with people like her coming and going. After more than a dozen failed attempts, she gave way to hunger and stopped at one of the beach concession stands. She would fill her empty stomach with some chow mein and Kung Pao chicken followed by a stroll on the beach. She found a great bathing suit in one of the hotel shops, changed out of her street clothes, stored her backpack in a rented locker, and was off to Waikiki. *Everything is perfect. It would be even more perfect if Curtis was here with me. Where did that come from? Isn't that the life I am trying to escape?* She took off her shoes and let the sand roll through her toes. The sand was hot, but not unbearable. The ocean looked inviting, and the palm trees that framed the beach were just what she had always imagined.

~ ~

A piercing pain shot through her foot. As she looked down to investigate the cause, she saw blood spilling onto the beach. She used her beach towel to wipe the sand from her foot and discovered that a sharp piece of coral had made a deep gash in the arch of her foot. A local stepped in to help. She had alcohol wipes in her day bag. She wiped the sand out of the cut, which stung a little, but was the right thing to do.

"You're gonna have to get that checked. You don't want your foot to get infected. There's a clinic about five blocks from here," the local said.

"Thank you, so much. I can't believe this would happen on my second walk on the beach," Rachel said.

19

It was a painful walk to the clinic followed by a bunch of questions Rachel really didn't want to answer. In the end, she yielded to filling out the forms that asked for her insurance. She was still covered on her parents insurance, but there would be a co-pay of twenty dollars. After another long wait sitting in a treatment room, someone finally stepped into the room.

"Hi, I'm Kalena. Let's take a look at that foot of yours." Kalena cleaned up the wound and used a medical version of Krazy Glue to hold the skin together. "You are very fortunate. If that cut had gone any deeper, it would have required stitches." Kalena then gave instructions about caring for the foot wound. "What's a young girl like you doing here all by yourself?"

"Looking for adventure!" Rachel replied.

"Looks like you've already found it," Kalena said with a smile. "If you are looking for more adventure, you should join me at church this Sunday."

"Adventure in church? Not in my world!" Rachel said. *I have been to church a lot of times but never found adventure*, she thought. One of the reasons she had left Idaho was to get away from church.

"Yes," Kalena replied, "Jesus said that He came that you might have life and have it in abundance."

OK, you're nice enough and I appreciate you helping me with my foot, but I'm outta here, Rachel thought. "Are we done now?" she questioned.

"Sure. Be careful to keep that foot covered in order to avoid infection. You may want to run some peroxide over it occasionally until it fully heals. I hope to see you in church someday. We meet Sundays at

20

ten o'clock. It's just a few blocks from here."

"Thanks again for your help," Rachel said.

As she walked out of the clinic a quiet voice spoke to her. *You asked Me for help and now you are walking away from it again.*

OK, Rachel responded, *but my biggest concern is getting a job, not going to some strange church.*

Immediately the voice said, *Go back in the clinic, and you'll find your job.*

Now there's an idea. I answered the phone for the chiropractor in Wilder. Maybe they need a receptionist. Can't hurt to ask.

~ ~

"Are you going to stare out that window all day?" Marie asked.

"I'm just hoping that one day Rachel is going to come walking up the driveway," Jake replied.

"I know, but staring out the window isn't going to make it happen."

"What do you expect me to do? I don't even know where she is right now. She could be anywhere."

"Well, instead of staring out the window, maybe we should get down on our knees," Marie suggested.

"You think I haven't been praying that she would come home? I've been praying every single day. Hardly a moment goes by that I don't worry about her and cast up another prayer," he protested.

"Well, maybe we should put some action to our prayers. Maybe we should do something."

"And what exactly would that be?"

"I don't know," Marie replied, as tears began to well up in her eyes. "I just don't know."

~ ~

The clinic business manager gave Rachel an application. Of course, a resume was an expected part of the process, and Rachel didn't know how she was going to make that happen. She was determined to pay cash for everything and didn't know if she could find an Internet café that would take cash. It would be hard to search for one on her gimpy foot. As she sat at the bus stop thinking she would go back to the airport, she thought, *I'll just Google it on my smart phone.* She found an Internet café just about a block from the clinic. When she walked into the café she thought, *What a godsend! They have it all here: computers, copying, Internet access, and a fax machine.*

Rachel walked up the counter. "I have a silly question. Do you accept cash payment for Internet access or time on the computers?"

"The easiest way is simply to use a credit card. If you don't have a credit or debit card you will have to purchase time on an access card. You can buy two hours for $6.95 or twenty-four hours for $14.95. There are a variety of software programs on the computers. The Internet access is included. If you need any help, I'll be just around the corner."

"I don't have my credit cards with me," Rachel said. "What do I do if I need to print something or make some copies?"

"I'll help you with that. Just come to the counter when you're ready."

I knew I could make things work, Rachel thought, trying to encourage herself. *Now let's create a resume that will make a real impression.* Not having much work experience, she knew would have to choose her words very carefully. No one was likely to be impressed with the fact that she worked one summer at the Wilder Chiropractic Office and weekends at Debbie's Diner. After she completed her very imaginative resume, she had it printed on linen paper. Rachel settled her bill and left the café feeling pretty proud of herself. She noted that she had just spent a couple days worth of meal money on twenty-five copies of a resume that may or may not land her a job. Another day in paradise ended with a bus trip to the airport and another uncomfortable night sleeping on a plastic bench. Her foot was starting to throb, and the idea of beach time the next day seemed impractical. What was she going to do with her time now that walking was not an option? The next several days seemed more like hell than paradise. There were no job openings available at the clinic. A waitressing job was out of the question until her foot healed. The clinic redressed her foot, which made beach time possible, but swimming in the ocean was risky. Maybe she would meet some interesting people at the beach. As each day passed, Rachel became more aware of the fact that her funds were quickly disappearing.

~ ~

Brook was trying to avoid any contact with Curtis, but in a town the size of Wilder that wasn't going to happen.

When Curtis walked into Debbie's Diner and saw her there, he asked, "Can I talk to you? How about moving over to a booth?"

She was more than happy to keep the coming conversation confidential. "What can I do for you?" she asked, as if she didn't already know.

"I heard you drove Rachel to the airport. How could you do that without giving me a heads up?" he chided.

"What difference does it make now?" she retorted. "It's not like you could have done anything about it. Her mind was made up."

"OK, this is not really getting us anywhere. I came to ask you if there is any way that I can get in touch with her."

"All I know is that she is in Hawaii somewhere. Have you tried calling or texting her? She has her phone," Brook suggested.

"I've tried, but she won't answer my calls or respond to my texts."

"Sorry. I truly am. I don't have any answers for you, and I need to get to work." Brook got up and went to the counter to pay.

Curtis sat in the booth and promised himself, *I'm going to find a way to get in touch with her and talk some sense into her.*

~ ~

Rachel's big break finally arrived. The business manager from the clinic called her about a job opening. The receptionist's family had relocated to the Big Island, and Kalena had suggested Rachel's name. After discussing a time for an interview with the manager, Rachel hung up her phone and thought, *There is a God in heaven. Where did that come from? Who cares? I've finally got a shot at keeping the adventure going.* She needed to get a good night's rest, a shower, and some presentable clothes for tomorrow's interview. It would take the last of her cash, but today she was going make an investment in herself. It was make it or break it time.

The interview went reasonably well, and thanks to Kalena's recommendation she was offered the job. She would start on Monday but wouldn't get paid for two weeks. She was thrilled and scared to death. She threw up a desperation prayer. *God help me. I know I don't deserve it, but if you can just get me through these next two weeks, I'll owe you.*

The still small voice she had come to know over the years spoke into her heart. *That's not the way I work. Try Kalena's church.*

Rachel reflected on the idea. *That's right; most churches have a food bank or something.*

She went back into the clinic to ask Kalena for directions to the church.

The church service that Sunday was amazing. She didn't know any of the worship choruses, but they were easy to sing and the worship band made things flow. Rachel was uplifted by the unusual setting. The church building was completely open air. There were no walls, just posts and a roof, and an incredible view of the Pacific Ocean. She felt sorry for the pastor. She wondered how he could keep them interested in his message with such a beautiful distraction. It was all so relaxed. Everyone was wearing comfortable island outfits. The people seemed so friendly. This wasn't the way she remembered church back home in Idaho, with hard, wooden pews, stuffy surroundings, and even stuffier people. *If only Mom and Dad could be here. They would love this stuff. Or maybe they would hate it. They actually liked the church in Idaho.*

After the service, Kalena greeted her with, "Did you enjoy the service?"

"It was great. I've never ever been to a church like this one," she replied.

"Would you like to join us for lunch? We are going down to Bubba Gumps."

"I appreciate the invite, but I can't afford it. Payday is two weeks away, and I'm totally broke. I was actually going to ask if your church had a food bank or something that can get me by until payday," Rachel said with embarrassment evident on her face.

"No problem. This will be my treat. You really have to try their pancakes with the vanilla bean syrup. It's as good as it gets."

As they talked over lunch, Kalena became aware that Rachel was sleeping at the airport. She invited Rachel to stay at her place until she got settled. It was the beginning of a great friendship – Rachel's first real friend in Hawaii.

~ ~

When prayer requests were taken at the end of the Bible study, Jake reminded everyone of their concern for Rachel. For months now the group had been faithfully praying for her safety and that she would come home.

"Something's gotta give here. She won't even accept our calls. We don't know where she is or even if she is all right. It's just not fair. She's breaking our hearts," Marie said, with her eyes once again welling up with tears.

"We're not giving up," Jake said. "We have to have faith. God is watching over her. God will bring her back home to us. I just know it."

~ ~

"You know that I love having you here. It's not about that. I just think that after three months it's about time that you find a place of your own," Kalena said.

"I know, I know. It's just that I'm really not ready to settle in. I don't want to sign a lease, and every place worth looking at requires at least six months," Rachel responded

"What's wrong with that?" Kalena shot back.

"What's wrong with that is that it would mean giving up on my dreams. I didn't come to Hawaii to get a job and an apartment. I came here looking for adventure," Rachel replied.

"And how are you going to find your adventure? What's it going to take to satisfy your need for excitement?"

"So, Kalena, that's a nice name. What does it mean? It's Hawaiian right?" Rachel asked, attempting to change the subject.

"What? What does my name mean? All right, my parents chose my name for a specific reason. It is a Hawaiian name for 'purity,'" she said.

"Of course it does. I always knew you were a goodie two-shoes," Rachel stated flatly.

"It has nothing to do with being good. The Lord knows there's nothing good in me. It has to do with purity. My parents have made it clear from the very beginning that only Christ can make me pure. His blood cleanses me, and His Spirit takes over from there."

"Well, it's also leaving you stuck in the mud. How pure is that? When are you going to add a little spice to your life?"

"If it's adventure you're looking for, I can tell you where to find it. Take a trip to the Big Island and talk to some of the YWAMers at the University of the Nations. They'll show you what real adventure is like," Kalena challenged.

"All right, when do I leave? I could use a little fun in my life. In fact, there's no time like the present. I just got paid, and now I don't have to pay any rent," she replied.

Rachel once again stepped away from someone who loved her in her quest for something just beyond her reach.

~ ~

"Would you quit looking out the window? You're driving me crazy," Marie exclaimed.

"I'm pretty sure I saw someone coming up the driveway. I think its Curtis. What's he doing here?" Jake asked.

Curtis knocked on the door and was quickly invited in.

"Hi, Curtis, how have you been? Can I get you a Coke or something?" Marie asked.

"No, thanks. I just came over to ask if you've heard from Rachel."

"Not a word. How about you? Have you heard from her?" Jake inquired.

"Nope, she's not even taking my calls. I wanted to tell her that I got the Simplot job. I start next month."

28

"Good for you!" Marie said.

"I should be thrilled, but without Rachel, what's the point?" *Who cares if I just found a really good job? It's not like it's going to make my life complete*, he thought.

"Curtis, you know that we love you. We are so sorry that Rachel just up and left. She left us too. I'm sorry we can't be more help," Jack said. "If you hear from her, would you let us know?"

Curtis told them that they would be his first call. Curtis had hoped to hear that Rachel had been in touch with her parents, but that obviously wasn't the case. *There's got to be some way to get in touch with her. I've got to figure this out*, he thought.

To be continued.

Searching For Paradise II

It wasn't until after Rachel arrived at the Kona airport that she discovered it was several miles into town. She was capable of making the seven-mile walk, but was neither in the mood to backpack into town nor pay twenty-five dollars for cab fare. She started walking down Highway 19 with her thumb out, hoping a tourist would find it in their heart to give her a lift. None were willing to stop on the desolate road. Even the gorgeous Hawaiian flora didn't seem to grow out here. It was hot and unusually dry for Hawaii. Finally, after she had walked several miles and was hot in body and attitude, a guy with a motorcycle stopped and asked if she needed a ride into town.

"I can't see that working," Rachel said. "Didn't you notice that I have a backpack?"

"Hi, my name is Cam, and you are?" Cameron said.

"I'm sorry, my name is Rachel. Thanks for stopping. So let's start over again. I'm hoping to catch a ride into Kona. I'm hot and bothered and just don't see how you can help."

"I can help on all counts. Keep the backpack on, throw a leg

30

over, and hang on tight. I'll give you a ride into town and you won't be hot or bothered anymore," he said with a smile.

"You don't even have a helmet for me."

"Helmets are not required here in Hawaii."

"How about you take me back to the airport and I'll get a locker for my backpack. Just take it slow until we get there."

"Sure, glad to help. Let's roll," Cam replied.

Rachel stopped in the restroom to change clothes, stored her backpack in a locker, and grabbed two Red Bulls.

"You like Red Bull?" she asked.

"Sure, I like mine with a little kick, but straight will be fine for now. So where are you from, Rachel? You don't look like a local," Cam observed.

"Really, and what do locals look like – grass skirts or a sarong?"

Cam grinned. "Nah, that sounds good. But it won't work on the bike. Are you ready to ride?"

"I'm ready as soon as you tell me two things. First, where are you from? And second, any chance you can bring me back to the airport at the end of the day?"

"I'm from Wisconsin, and yes, I promise to bring you back here if that's what you really want. How about we take a run up to Kilauea and see what's hot besides you," Cam said with a smirk.

"You've been in the sun too long, Cam. Let's go into Kona, get something to eat, and take a walk on the beach. By the way, if you're from Wisconsin, how did you get your motorcycle to the island?" Rachel questioned.

"Oh, this isn't mine. I rented it for a couple days. I just wanted to really see the island, and there's no better way than on a bike."

"Wow, that's pretty smart for a guy from Wisconsin," Rachel teased.

"OK. Are you sure you really want to start this?" he challenged. "So where are you from? Just come off the farm?"

"Close enough. A ranch in Idaho. Let's ride."

As they rolled out of the airport, Rachel put her arms around Cam. It took her back to her last ride with Curtis. She wished she had her arms around Curtis rather than this stranger from Wisconsin. *Why do I always go there? I've made my choice and it's Hawaii, not Idaho*, she reminded herself.

They had a nice lunch in downtown Kona, enjoyed the afternoon walking along the beach, and watching the waves break on the rocks along the shore. It was peaceful and relaxing right up until the point when Cam suggested that they have a Mai Tai.

"I'm not old enough to drink," Rachel said.

"Hey, don't worry about it, pretty girl. I'm old enough, and I'll order two and walk them down to the beach."

Rachel had come looking for adventure, but she wasn't about to get drunk with the first guy she met. She would have to think of something fast.

"You know, I'm pretty new at riding on a bike, and I'm not ready to ride on the back of a bike with someone who's been drinking. Let's save that idea for another time when I don't need a ride back to the airport."

"Hey, no one said you had to go back to the airport. We could get a room and go back for your backpack tomorrow."

Rachel got his drift and jumped right into her defense mode. "You promised to take me back to the airport. Is that a promise you intend to keep, or do I need to call a cab?"

Cam could see that he had crossed a line with this one and was interested enough to back off. He suggested they tour the island tomorrow on the bike.

Rachel saw an opportunity to step back from Cam's advances. "Sounds good. How about you take me back to the airport, and we'll figure out tomorrow's agenda?" Another night on an airport bench didn't sound appealing, but neither did spending the night with Cam. Paradise was filled with dilemmas Rachel had never imagined. They agreed to meet at nine just outside the airport terminal.

Cam rolled up the next morning and suggested a full circle tour around the island, including Kilauea lava fields, the black sands beach, Rainbow waterfall, and Waipio Valley. It sounded like fun to Rachel, but she said they had to get back in time for worship at the University of the

Nations.

This caught Cam by surprise. "Worship? Are you talking about some kind of Hawaiian cultural thing with ukuleles or something? What is this University of the Nations thing?"

"No," Rachel responded, "just something that a friend from Oahu said I shouldn't miss."

"OK, if you say so. Where is this University of the Nations?"

"Just outside of Kona. We can Google it when we get back to this side of the island. Let's hit the road."

Everything was perfect. Rachel could feel the freedom she was looking for as the wind blew through her hair. Every stop was extraordinary, and Cam was a lot of fun. The Anuenue Shave Ice at Kamuela was an unexpected surprise. They had the most delicious ice cream in every imaginable flavor. Rachel chose toasted coconut and Cam had caramel macadamia nut. The Kona coffee was the best she had ever tasted. Finally Rachel was starting to experience a part of her dreams. She was leaving Idaho behind and welcoming a whole new world.

When they pulled into the University of the Nations' parking lot, Cam wanted to beg off of this part of the trip. Rachel won him over by saying Kalena had said it was a sure fire hit and it would probably be a great way to complete the island tour. Cam reluctantly agreed.

When it was over Cam said, "Kalena was right. That was incredible. It was a like a rock concert with people singing and the band just lighting it up. This is what you call church? It's not like any church I've ever seen."

"Christianity out here in Hawaii is nothing like back home in Idaho."

34

"So you're a Christian?" Cam asked.

"Well, not really. At least not like this. These people seem to really get it."

Just then a couple of YWAMers walked up and greeted them.

"Hi, I'm Gino. You guys just arrive?"

"Well, I've been in Hawaii for a couple of months, but just arrived on the Big Island yesterday," Rachel responded.

Cam said he had been on the island for three days.

"Are you guys YWAMers?"

"No," Rachel and Cam said in unison.

"Well, welcome to the island. Have you got any plans for tomorrow? We have the day off from school, and some of us are going snorkeling at Kamakahonu, also known as Children's Beach. You wanna come?"

"I would love to," Rachel said. "I'm always looking for a good place to lie in the sun, but what I really need is a place to stay the night."

"Hey, you guys can crash in my room. But only for one night. We're technically not supposed to have people stay in our rooms. We can head down to the beach in the morning," Gino suggested.

The next morning Gino loaded up the snorkeling gear and a day bag. Rachel knew she was going to need to buy another suit, as hers was in the backpack at the airport. Gino asked the girls if they could set her up with something. One of the girls had something that was a little baggy and way too conservative. *Oh well, it'll have to do,* she thought. They drove off to Kamakahonu Beach with Cam and Rachel following on the bike. Cam had his beach towel, swimsuit and sunscreen in the saddlebag.

When they got to the beach, their new friends were quick to set them up with snorkeling gear.

"You want to put the water socks on right now. It's quite a ways out to the snorkeling depth and the rocks are very slippery. You don't have to worry about the tide or any waves. This beach has a sea barrier, so it's one of the safest beaches on the island. You are going to see some phenomenal schools of tropical fish. Have either one of you ever snorkeled before?" Gino asked.

"No. There's not a lot of snorkeling in Idaho," Rachel said.

"It's really easy. Just be aware of when your snorkel goes under water. Each time you come up, blow out real hard and clear the snorkel. It's just like a whale spouting when they come up from the ocean. So go ahead and enjoy," he said.

Off they went past the slippery rocks into the warm ocean water. When the water reached waist deep, they put the fins, mask and snorkel on and entered a world of enchantment. The schools of fish were mind-boggling. Cam had done his share of fishing in Wisconsin, but this was way different. The kaleidoscope of colors was unlike anything he had

ever seen. They glided from one astonishing school of fish to another. The highlight of the day was when a huge sea turtle floated right up next to them.

I've never seen anything so incredible in my life. I'm not sure that I want to get out of the water. I could stay here for a lifetime, Rachel thought. She knew there were others waiting on the beach to get their chance to join the excitement, so she reluctantly followed Cam's signal to head back. When she came out of the water, she was so grateful to Gino for inviting them on this snorkeling adventure that she couldn't help but give him a huge hug.

Cam looked over and was surprised at the twinge of jealousy he felt. He quickly handed Gino the snorkeling gear and said, "Next. Hey, Rachel, are you hungry? Maybe we can find a little snack shop or something."

"I'm starved and exhausted. Let's see what we can find," she replied.

After lunch most of the gang hung out on the beach. Rachel was glad to catch some rays. She loved the sun and was really pleased that she was getting her very first real tan. *Boy wouldn't the gang in Idaho be jealous*, she pondered. *In Wilder you would pay a fortune for a tan like this.*

After coming back from his snorkeling time, Gino said, "Isn't God's creation terrific? I can't believe the artistry He has worked into His creation."

"So you think God created all this?" Cam questioned.

"Of course He did. You think this all just happened because of some cosmic big bang?"

"Actually I do, and it's not just me. Every science teacher I've ever known agrees with me," Cam retorted.

"OK. But I think when you were out there in this astounding place, your heart told you something special brought it all together," Gino suggested.

"Close. I was amazed at how beautiful it was. So what?" Cam questioned.

"So your heart was telling you that this couldn't have happened by a cosmic accident. In your heart you know there is a God."

"You know, you guys can spout all the trash you want. I'm not buying into all this God stuff."

"Fine. But there are more people in this world who agree with me than disagree."

"That's fine with me, and I'm going to go find some of them and party. I'm outta here. You coming Rachel?" Cam said, as he began to gather his towel and head for the bike.

"It's not like I have a choice," Rachel said. "You're my ride back to the airport."

Gino stepped up next to Cam and said, "I'm sorry, man. Maybe I was a little too strong in what I said and how I said it. Hang in here and enjoy the beach."

"Right you are, man. Rachel, are you coming or not?"

"Rachel, you can go or stay, but don't feel that you don't have options. We'll take you to the airport if you want," Gino said.

Rachel turned to Cam and said, "Why don't you calm down, and we can take another swim in the ocean."

"No thanks. Been there and done that. I'm on to bigger and better things. I've got to get this bike back the rental shop. You coming?"

"No, I don't think I will. I came to Hawaii to live it up, and this beach is about as good as it gets," she said.

"Fine. If you really want to live it up, you can find me at the End of the Road on Kauai."

Gino came over to Rachel and apologized. "I didn't mean to offend him. I was simply trying to let him know that there are more people who believe there is a god than those who disbelieve. I don't know how you can see all the wonderful things in creation and not realize that there is a Creator.

"He can think and do whatever he wants. I'm here to have a good time, and I'm not going to let him or anyone else take that away from me," Rachel declared. "What was he talking about when he said I could find him at the End of the Road?"

"The End of the Road is on the north side of Kauai. It's up west of Princeville. The road on that side of the island literally ends as the mountains cut right down into the ocean. I don't want to get into the specifics, but there's a lot of bad stuff that goes on there."

"Hey, I'm here looking for adventure. Sounds like there's a party going on there."

"It's not the kind of adventure you should be looking for," Gino stated, emphatically.

"Who are you to tell me where I should be looking for adventure? Come to think of it, Kalena said that if I was looking for adventure that I should talk to one of you YWAMers. What was she talking about?" Rachel asked.

"I don't really know what Kalena was talking about, but I'm pretty sure that there are a couple of options when it comes to adventure: one where you are looking for adventure apart from God, and one where you find adventure with God. I've tried both and I know which one is working for me. I started my adventure with God a few years ago, and I wouldn't look back."

"Adventure with God? Really? The best I can do is to try to keep from falling asleep when I go to church," she said.

"So were you falling asleep last night? Looked to me like you were wide awake and having a good time."

"Yeah, but that wasn't church. I don't know what that was, but it wasn't like any church where I've ever been."

"I'm not talking about church. I'm talking about walking with God. I'm talking about a relationship with God. That's what leads to adventure," he said with passion.

"And what kind of adventures have you been on with God?" she questioned.

"Every day is an adventure with Him. But you probably want to know where I've been and what I've seen. He led me here first of all, and then on some mission trips to Delhi, Indonesia, and on a Mercy ship near Thailand after the tsunami hit."

"What did you do there?"

"Well, in Delhi we helped feed some very poor people, in Indonesia we taught some children about Jesus and shared a film each night, and in Thailand we helped them recover from the tsunami."

"So going around the world being a good guy is your idea of adventure?" she asked somewhat sarcastically.

"I guess so, if that's the way you see it. But I would rather say it this way: I go anywhere God sends me, try to do whatever He asks me to do, and get to watch what He's doing when He shows up to meet people's needs."

"OK, preacher man, but the adventure I'm looking for is another swim with the sea turtle. You up to that?" she asked, as she reached for

40

the snorkel gear. She didn't want to admit it, but Gino was making her think.

"You're on. Let's hit the water."

When they came out of the water over an hour later, Rachel was exhausted, content, and hungry again. It had been a full day and she needed to get something to eat and find a place to sleep.

When she explained her concerns to Gino, another member of the group said, "I know the custodian at the Trade Winds Community Church. He let me take some friends there when they were visiting Kona. Let me check and see if he can find a spot for you."

She picked up her cell phone and gave the custodian a call, explained Rachel's situation, and asked if he could make a spot for her for one night. He said they had a cot she could use. The property was fenced in and he would be leaving by nine. They would have to make it there before then.

"We'll be there to drop her off."

Mahalo God, Rachel silently responded. *These people are terrific.*

They had supper together and dropped Rachel off at the church. The custodian showed her around. The cot was in a place that had a roof but no walls. He said that the weather looked good and that he would lock the gate when he left.

That night she recounted the events and discussions of the day. She was amazed at all she had seen and heard. The beach was perfect. She hadn't even dreamed of getting to swim right next to a sea turtle, and the tropical fish were incredible. *Maybe Gino was right. Maybe there had to be a creator behind all I had witnessed.* She didn't know about

41

the rest of it. The whole adventure with God thing was interesting, but she still had some exploring to do in the adventure realm. Tomorrow she was going to find a way to get to the End of the Road.

~ ~

Curtis walked up to the door, knocked twice, and heard Marie invite him in.

"Hi, Curtis, good to see you," she said.

"Good to see you too. I thought I had better stop by and fill you in before I left."

"Where are you going?"

"Hawaii. I'm going looking for Rachel. I'm tired of waiting, and I just believe she's in trouble."

"Trouble? What do you mean you think she's in trouble?"

"I don't know. I just sense it. I feel it deep inside."

"Have you heard something? Did Brook tell you something?"

"No, I don't know what it is. I just know I have to find her," Curtis responded.

"Let me get Jake in here. He's just outside. Jake! Jake! Can you come in here for a minute?" Marie shouted.

Jake came in wondering what the fuss was all about, and could see the concern written on Marie's face. When he saw Curtis sitting at the table, he assumed something bad had happened.

"Curtis, what are you doing here?" he asked.

"I came to tell you I am leaving for Hawaii. I am going to go find Rachel and try to convince her to come home."

"Tell him the rest," Marie interjected.

"I just believe that she's in some kind of trouble," Curtis said.

"What makes you say that?"

"I don't have any reason to say that, other than somehow I can sense it."

"So what's your plan? What are you going to do?" Jake asked.

"I don't know. I figured that you would know something, and I would start there. I'm going to try and track her down."

"All we know is that she was seen at the Urgent Care Clinic of Waikiki about three months ago. We received an Explanation of Benefits form from our insurance company. We haven't heard anything since," Jake explained.

"Well, that's a start."

"Are you sure about this? It sounds like a fool's journey," Jake stated.

"I've got to do something, anything. I just can't sit here and wonder and worry."

"I don't think this will work, but God knows we want her to come home. We'll write you a check for her plane ticket home just in case you actually find her and can convince her to come home."

"Thanks. That will help a lot. I'll call you when I get to Honolulu."

"When are you going to leave?" Marie asked.

"Tomorrow. I'm going to check with Brook to see if she knows anything."

"We'll be praying for you. Please keep us informed every step of the way," Jake said.

Curtis then went looking for Brook. He checked all over town before he found her at the Jackson's gas station. He pulled up next to her car, rolled down his window and said, "I've got to get in touch with Rachel. I know that she contacts you. Brook, I really need you to tell me what you know."

"So you want me to break confidence with my friend?"

"No, I want you to lend me a hand so I can help her."

"What makes you think she needs your help?"

"Listen, I don't know what to tell you. I just know that she needs me, and you are the only one who might be able point me in her direction so I can be there for her."

"And just how do you expect to do that?"

"Just tell me where she is. I'm going to go find her and convince her to come home."

"I don't know much. The last time she texted me she told me about swimming with the sea turtles at Children's Beach," Brook said in a frustrated tone. "That's all I know."

"Thanks, Brook. You won't regret this," he promised.

"We'll see about that. If Rachel finds out that I told you I'll probably lose her as a friend forever."

~ ~

Rachel got up early the next morning, found her way to Highway 19, and hitched a ride to the airport. She used her paycheck money to buy a ticket to Kauai. After she bought breakfast at the food court, she had less than ten dollars left. That didn't leave many options once she got to

Kauai. But she was determined to get to the next stop on her great adventure. The flight to Kauai flew past the Kilauea volcano and made a quick stopover connection in Honolulu. As she waited for her backpack at baggage claim in Lihue Airport, she asked around about the End of the Road. Most of the tourists didn't have any idea, but someone suggested she ask an agent at the ticket counter. She found an agent who knew the island.

"Why would a pretty, young girl like you be interested in the End of the Road?" he asked.

"I'm looking for adventure, and I have a friend who said he was headed up there."

"To each his or her own, but that place is trouble. It has a reputation for drugs. I hear reports about the cops having to clean the place out all the time," the agent warned her.

"I'm just asking for directions," Rachel said impatiently.

"You can catch the bus right outside here. Tell the driver that you want to go to Hanalei. He'll give you some help. You'll have to make several changes. I hope you have some rain gear. It rains quite a bit on the north side of the island. Once you get to Hanalei you will have to hitch a ride down to End of the Road."

"Thanks," Rachel replied, and headed out of the terminal.

The bus ride was gorgeous. She had a view of the ocean time and time again. The palm trees were more majestic than on the other islands. It took less than an hour to get to Hanalei. She used half of her remaining cash to buy lunch and took a short walk to Highway 560 where she picked up a ride to the End of the Road. She was on her way. When she arrived, she thought, *This is nothing like the ticket agent described.*

Everyone always has to be so negative. This looks like heaven. She went looking for Cam, which might have been a mistake. There were a variety of people on Tunnels Beach. Most of them were having a good time. There were people snorkeling, others tanning on the beach. There were small groups of what looked like homeless people. They didn't appear to be very friendly. Rachel was hoping to find Cam and meet some new Hawaiian friends. She asked one of the people tanning where she could change.

"Right here."

"No, I meant, where is the nearest restroom?"

"You aren't going to find one of those on this beach. You can take a short hike in the jungle, or there are some caves in that direction."

Rachel chose the caves, which didn't work out as well as she would have liked. There were more homeless-type beach people hanging out in the cave, but it was a big cave and she found a dark area where she could change. She found a place to hide her backpack near the cave and headed for the water. She decided that it was a good time to take a swim. She was a little put off by the posted sharks and riptide warning signs, but there were others in the water, so it couldn't be that dangerous. The water was

46

as warm and beautiful as on the other islands.

Hawaii is magnificent, she thought. *I'm so glad I came here.* After a long swim, she laid out her beach towel and soaked in the rays. For some reason, she started to feel cold. *Time to go back to the cave to get into something warm*, she thought. She discovered that a lot of people had the same idea. The cave was crowded, and there were many lighting up. The air in the cave was filled with the smell of cigarette and marijuana smoke. *People could almost get high on the secondhand smoke*, she thought.

She walked over to someone that looked safe and asked if there were any street vendors near the beach.

"You must be a tourist. Everyone knows that you don't come to this beach without bringing your own food. The nearest restaurant is in Hanalei, five miles down the road."

Rachel explained that she was really hungry and didn't have much money.

"You could walk into the mountains and look for fruit trees, but you'll find it is pretty picked over."

Desperation moved Rachel out of the cave. She headed into the jungle looking for anything she could find. She found some trees and bushes that had some kind of fruit on them. She wondered if they were truly edible, or possibly poisonous. She sampled a little of each potential fruit she found. After an hour of searching she realized that this wasn't solving the problem, so she headed down the mountain and back to the cave.

It's time to settle in, she thought.

The cave was packed with people trying to do the same thing.

The tourists had gotten into their cars and headed off to what she assumed was a warm and dry bed. *That would sure be nice,* she thought. Her foam rollup and sleeping bag wasn't providing much comfort, but it kept her off the cold, rock floor of the cave. Her beach towel served as her pillow once again, but to be honest it was a long, cold, uncomfortable night. In addition to the discomfort of the cold floor of the cave, Rachel struggled to overcome the irritating sound of roosters that seemed to crow all through the night. When morning broke, the rain had cleared and most had left the cave. There were small fires at the edges of the beach as people were trying to fashion some sort of breakfast. Anything sounded good to Rachel. Her $3.65 wouldn't provide much, even if there had been a place to get something.

I've got to think here. I have to find something to eat, or I will have to go back into town and find a job. I've got enough cash to take the bus back to Lihue, but then I wouldn't have enough money left for food. Even if I found a job, how would I survive without food until I got a paycheck? Nearby, a rooster crowed and interrupted her thought process. *That's it. I'm an Idaho girl. I know how to catch a chicken. I'll catch one of those roosters and have enough meat for the whole day. OK, first I have to ask the locals about how I can get a fire going. Time for action.*

Rachel went from one group that had a fire to the next until she finally found one friendly enough to share the information she needed. Finding dry wood was going to be a challenge after yesterday's rain. Even if she were able to gather what she needed, she didn't have any matches or a lighter. She found enough wood for a small fire and hid it from view in a place near the beach. *Now comes the real challenge – catching one of those blasted roosters.* It wasn't hard to find them. They

48

were constantly crowing and didn't seem to be wary of people. Rachel gathered some rocks that seemed suitable for the task. She felt like David going after Goliath but without a sling. Fortunately she had a good arm, and after several foiled attempts she finally hit the mark. A quick wring of the neck and she was good to go. *Pluck the feathers, start the fire, and voila I'll be eating chicken for lunch,* she thought, commending herself for her ingenuity. She pulled out her Leatherman tool and used the knife to shape a spit and carefully shave a skewer. It wouldn't be Chick-fil-A, but at least she had something to eat. Finding a lighter among the groups wasn't too difficult. They were willing to share, though she noted they watched her carefully until she returned with the lighter. It took longer to barbecue the rooster than she had thought, and the meat was unbelievably tough. *Beggars can't be choosers,* she reminded herself.

She watched the fire burn out, hid her backpack in the trees, dropped the remains of the rooster in the garbage bin, and headed for the ocean. As she walked past one of the groups gathered around a fire, a pit bull charged her. It charged full speed to the end of its chain and viciously stayed in attack mode until she moved away. *Even Paradise has its share of garbage,* she thought. *I can't believe they can get away with having a dog like that in a place like this.*

One of the things she hadn't planned for was showers. The ocean water left her skin with a salted covering, which made her chafe. Rachel couldn't believe all the things that she had left out of her wonderful plans for paradise. The ocean water was terrific. There were schools of tropical fish that were visible even without goggles, and they floated past just above the coral reef. In spite of the remarkable setting, Rachel's sense of dissatisfaction was growing. It wasn't that she wasn't enjoying herself.

Even the challenge of finding food brought some satisfaction. No, it was the sense of being alone. There was no one with whom she could share this great experience. *Curtis would probably love this. He would rent a motorcycle, roll around the island and take in every moment*, she thought. *What is this obsession with Curtis? I guess I can't sweep him out of my mind as easily as I thought.*

Suddenly she felt a cramping in her stomach. She assumed it was related to swimming too soon after eating. She had been warned about that, but had believed that it was just an old wives' tale. It was time to get ashore, lie down on the beach, and work on her tan. As she laid out her beach towel, the cramping increased. The sun felt unusually hot for this time of day. *Maybe I should find a place in the shade and get something to drink.* Something to drink was another provision she had not made for this trip. She walked over to the group that had lent her the lighter, thinking they might have some water they might share. As she approached the group, she collapsed in the sand.

Sometime later, she awoke in what seemed to be the cave. She wondered how she had gotten there.

As she lifted her head, someone said, "Lie still. You need to rest."

"What's going on? Where am I?" Rachel asked.

"You're in the Tunnels Beach cave. You passed out, and we carried you here. We've called for an ambulance."

"I don't have any money. I can't afford an ambulance," Rachel weakly responded.

"You don't have a choice, girl. They're already on the way. What's your name? Where are you from?"

"Rachel Martin. I used to live in Idaho. Why do I feel so horrible?"

"Someone saw you trying to roast one of our roosters. You know, it's illegal to kill those roosters. Those things will make you sick every time. You should have asked us about them before you gave it a try."

When the ambulance arrived, Rachel was loaded onto a gurney and driven to the North Shore Medical Center.

~ ~

Curtis arrived in Honolulu on a mission. He was going to find Rachel and convince her to come home. His first stop was going to be the Urgent Care Clinic of Waikiki. He hailed a cab and instructed the driver of his destination.

When he walked into the clinic he went up to the reception desk and said, "I'm looking for Rachel Martin. I know that she was here three months ago for some kind of treatment."

"Are you family?" the receptionist asked.

"I'm a friend from Idaho. I came here looking for her," Curtis replied.

Fortunately Kalena was stationed just around the partition and heard Rachel's name. She came to the front desk and asked who was looking for Rachel.

"I am," Curtis responded. "I'm her boyfriend from Idaho."

"She told me about you. She stayed at my place for a few months," Kalena said.

51

"Can you tell me where to find her?"

"All I know is she was headed for the University of the Nations on the Big Island. That's the last we have heard from her."

"How do I get there?"

"You will have to fly there. Once you get to the airport on the Big Island, just tell them you're looking for the YWAM base. It's not too far from the airport."

"Thanks. You've been very helpful. I've gotta run!" Curtis said as he quickly exited the building.

"I wonder what that was all about," Kalena said reflectively.

The flight to the Big Island of Hawaii was beautiful, not that Curtis noticed. His mind was too focused on his mission and trying to figure out what he would find at the University of the Nations. He knew his chances of finding Rachel were very slim, but his heart was pressing him forward. His first stop at the YWAM base was the Admissions office. They didn't have a Rachel Martin registered and didn't know anything about her. There were always people passing through, but they didn't usually check in with the office. Curtis walked the campus and questioned every person he could find. They were all friendly enough, but after searching all afternoon he was about ready to give up. By God's grace, he ran into someone who thought they had met Rachel. She had gone snorkeling with them at Children's Beach.

"That's her!" Curtis exclaimed. "Brook said she went to Children's Beach."

"You need to talk to Gino. He's the one who talked with her the most."

"Where's Gino?"

"He should be in the cafeteria. I'll take you there."

Gino told Curtis about their conversation, including the fact they had talked about the End of the Road on Kauai. Gino shared that he had warned her about that place, but she left the next morning without talking to anyone. They all assumed that she had left for Kauai.

~ ~

As the ambulance took Rachel to the hospital, the only thing she could think about was her inability to pay for all this. *I would get out right now if they would let me off without a bill.* She knew that wasn't how it worked. When she arrived at the North Shore Medical Center, they lifted her off the gurney and onto the exam table. She tried to get off the table and nearly passed out again.

A doctor came to examine her, rolled through the usual preliminary questions and then asked, "So what happened?"

Rachel told him that she didn't have any money and was hungry, about her search for fruit and nuts in the mountains, and killing and cooking the rooster. She apologized for doing something illegal and said that she really didn't know it was against the law or that eating them would make her sick.

The doctor smiled and said, "It's not illegal to kill those roosters. They won't make you sick unless you don't cook them well enough. What I think we have here is a serious case of food poisoning. We'll run some tests. If I'm right we'll give you an IV with fluids and some nausea and pain medicine. We'll get you through this. You'll be fine and probably be out of here in a day or so."

"You don't understand. I don't have any money. I can't afford to be here. I shouldn't have even come here," Rachel stated.

"We'll work all that out once you get past this. For now you need to try to get some rest," the doctor said.

~ ~

When Curtis arrived at Lihue Airport, he went to the car rental area. It was a tough decision whether he should rent a car by the day or for a full week. In the end he decided to choose a full week. He figured Rachel was most likely on Kauai, and he wasn't going to stop looking until he found her. When his turn came at the counter, he discovered that he wasn't old enough to rent a car. He asked the rental agent how he might get to the End of the Road.

The agent gave him a concerned look and said, "You can catch the bus just outside the terminal and make connections to Hanalei. From there you will have to hitch a ride and that's no easy task."

"I have to go there, so can you get me pointed in the right direction?"

"Go right through those doors, look for the Kauai Bus Line sign, and tell the driver you want to go to Hanalei."

"Thanks," Curtis said, and quickly exited the terminal. When he got to the bus stop he prayed, *God, You know where Rachel is and what I need to do to find her. Would you please help me with this impossible mission?*

God spoke softly into his heart. *Have faith, Curtis. Nothing is impossible for Me.*

That truth ran through his mind all the way up the coast to Hanalei. He noticed the astonishing ocean views that flowed past the window, but his mind was too focused on finding Rachel to really enjoy them.

~ ~

When Rachel's cramping lessened and the cold sweats finally went away, she began to ask questions: What am I going to wear? How in the world am I going to be able to pay my medical bill? When will I be able to leave? Will my backpack still be where I left it? What happened to my cell phone? What am I going to do about food?

Believe it or not she was actually enjoying the food the medical center was providing. She began to think about how much she missed her home, especially her bed and favorite pillow. When a physician's assistant came in to see her, Rachel asked a selective set of what she believed would be safe questions. The answer to the first question was that she needed to stay for observation for at least one more day. The PA assured Rachel that the staff could find some clothes that would fit. Also, they would need an address and a phone number before she could be released. Rachel explained that she was visiting Hawaii, which raised the question of her place of residence. She had a phone number, but her phone was in her backpack at Tunnels Beach. She was willing to provide her parents' address in Wilder as long as they didn't contact them directly. The PA said that she would look into these issues with the business manager and get back to her. As the PA left, Rachel offered up a quick prayer. *God, if You can find a way to get me out of the mess I've made, get me back home and help my parents forgive me for running off like this, I'll never complain again. I promise.* She was physically and emotionally exhausted, and it was really taking a toll. She welcomed the chance to simply sleep in a warm and comfortable bed.

~ ~

Curtis finally reached Tunnels Beach at the End of the Road. He started his search by moving from one small group to another asking about Cam and Rachel. After roaming the beach in a relentless pursuit, someone suggested that he try the caves. They mentioned that some of the people who made this beach their home hung out there. What Curtis found at the cave confirmed his worst fears. It was clear that some of the people were on drugs. Nonetheless, he pressed on asking every person he could find. He couldn't picture Rachel being comfortable with any of these people, but he wasn't about to quit now. He left the cave and returned to the beach. He decided to try calling Rachel's cell phone. She hadn't been taking his calls, but maybe he could hear it ring and find her that way. *Unbelievable,* he thought when he heard a phone ringing. He followed the sound to a place just off the beach. When he found her cell phone in a backpack, his hope began to rise. He started searching the area around her backpack thinking she couldn't have gone far. She wouldn't have willingly left it unattended. He continued to search and call out her name. One of the beach bums had sobered up enough to remember the events of the previous day.

"I think her name was Rachel," he told Curtis. He asked around, and a couple others said they thought he was right. He told about her collapsing on the beach and the ambulance picking her up.

That was enough to get Curtis moving. He grabbed Rachel's backpack, got back on the road, and headed toward Hanalei. He hoped someone there would know exactly where the ambulance had taken Rachel. The clerk at the county courthouse told him the ambulance would most likely have gone to North Shore Medical Center and said that the bus would be able to drop him off within a short walking distance of the center.

When he arrived at the medical center, he asked the receptionist if Rachel Martin was there. She took Curtis to Rachel's room. Rachel was asleep, so Curtis sat in a chair beside her bed and thanked God for coming through with the impossible. When Rachel awoke and saw Curtis at her bedside, she thought she was dreaming.

He took her hand and said, "Are you all right?"

She knew then it wasn't a dream. It was an answer to her prayer. She told Curtis about praying that God would get her out of this mess and find a way to get her home.

"That's why I came here," Curtis said. "There's one thing you have to do. You need to call your parents and let them know that you are all right." Curtis dialed the number and handed her his cell phone.

~ ~

When Marie heard Rachel's voice on the phone, she literally lost her breath.

"Mom, are you all right?"

"I'm fine. I'm just so glad to hear from you. Are you all right?"

"I'm better now, Mom. I'm so sorry. I'm so sorry for leaving the way I did. Can you ever forgive me?" Rachel said with a catch in her voice.

"Nothing to forgive, hon. Just please come home."

"There's no place I'd rather be. Curtis is here. He came to find me," Rachel said with gratitude in her voice.

When Marie finally hung up the phone, she literally screamed with excitement, which brought Jake into the house wondering what in the world was going on.

"She's coming home. Our baby girl is coming home," Marie exclaimed.

With tears in their eyes, Jake and Marie knelt on the kitchen floor and gave thanks to God for answering their prayers.

Premonition

The harshness of the bright spotlight assaulted his eyes, and the reflected red and blue lights contrasted with his black and white surroundings as the rain continued to fall on the wet asphalt. Smoke - no steam resembling smoke - rose from somewhere toward the front of his car. Beside him in the seat was a woman. He could not remember her name. She was leaning forward against the seat belt restraint. Her head had fallen forward, and her short, curly blond hair was caked with blood and broken glass. A thin line of blood issued from her ear and followed her jaw line to her chin where it had begun to drip into her lap. She made no sound. He was unable to perceive any movement of her chest that might indicate she was breathing.

There were sounds foreign to him as movement outside the car indicated emergency personnel were working with heavy equipment trying to gain access through the crushed metal of the doors. He felt no pain or discomfort despite the pummeling his face received when the airbag deployed. Like a foggy mirror steamed by a hot shower, his mind couldn't produce a clear picture of what had just happened.

He struggled to recount the events that preceded this moment in time. The metal of the passenger side door groaned as it was finally taken away. He recognized the shoulder patch of the young man leaning in as that of an EMT.

The flicker of a small flashlight as he opened her eyelids, then three fingers pressed along her neck, were followed by a soft exclamation filled with pain, "She's gone."

Gone? Gone as in dead? Gone as in never to laugh, smile, or watch children play in the park? Gone as in to never have the opportunity to marry and grow old with someone she loved? Gone as in gone forever?

~ ~

As he combed his hair, he looked closely at his reflected image in the bathroom mirror. He took pride in what he saw. He was not really handsome, but reasonably good looking with a straight nose, clear brown eyes, and a strong chin. His teeth were straight and white, and the smile that displayed them was always ready to be shared with those around him. At twenty-six, already more than a quarter of a century had come and gone since the doctor had slapped his butt to encourage his breathing.

Born of educated, upper middle-class parents, he was an only child. The possibility of the kinship of brothers and sisters was forfeited by his parents' desire for successful careers. Somewhere just below the surface he had always held resentment that they had deprived him of the one thing he truly wanted. Somehow cutting-edge electronics, designer clothing, and fine food fell short when he watched friends scuffle with their siblings or recount their time around the table at Thanksgiving and Christmas.

College held little interest for him. He knew he did not need to establish himself or search for success. He knew he was the sole heir to whatever family fortunes the diligence of his parents had provided. He attended college so he could enjoy the social life and was able to maintain reasonable grades by picking and choosing his subjects carefully. None of the classes pointed toward a career or gave him any great sense of accomplishment. He felt he was just treading water, waiting for a door to open and reveal something he should passionately pursue. The same was true of the women in his life. He enjoyed their companionship, the interaction, and occasionally the physical dimension of the relationship. But he did not focus on it like many of his friends.

Dexter felt like a casual observer, almost a non-participant in his own life, which seemed to operate quite well without his guidance or attention. Sometimes he mused at how events seemed to set his course without his assent. He wondered, then dismissed the idea that someone or something greater than himself was in charge. Neither Dexter nor his parents had the time or inclination to pursue religion. They were seemingly content to enjoy what they thought of as the fruits of their own labors.

~ ~

As a freshman and barely nineteen, Gretchen enjoyed the freedom of being away from home for the first time. She had grown up in the small, eastern Washington town of Walla Walla and was thrilled to be attending Oregon State University. She had selected OSU because of the great setting and its reputation as a very good veterinary college. With fewer than 60,000 in population, Corvallis was a much better fit for her than Portland or Seattle. She especially liked the easy access to her favorite outdoor activities. Snowboarding, canoeing, trail rides, and long hikes into the mountains were just minutes away from her campus. To Gretchen, life was full of challenge, mystery and promise. Each day seemed to bring excitement and new discovery.

Veterinary medicine was a good fit for her as well. Her grades in math and science and the potential to provide for the animals she loved had helped her narrow her options. She pictured herself back home someday helping to birth a foal, or diagnosing the cause of a dog's pain. She found it more interesting to learn the health needs of several species than to jump into the health care industry, which had a singular focus.

She smirked when she asked her prof, "How does one tell if an iguana has a fever?"

She did not think of herself as a prude, but as a common-sense Christian woman who tried hard to make good choices. Her friends knew that she could be trusted to be their designated driver if they needed a ride home. Her family's income had been stretched just enough to allow her to attend college without being forced to maintain a side job. Sundays she could be found at the University Chapel. She was often part of the worship team. Each week a small group would gather after the service to discuss the sermon and pray for the needs of others. She would often stay and join them.

~ ~

As he entered the library, Dexter's attention was drawn to her like the proverbial moth to the flame. She sat with several others laughing and nodding. *She is young*, he thought to himself, *just out of high school*. What was it about her that drew his attention? On the table in front of them he could see an array of books. Not just books but Bibles and most of them open. *So, am I looking at a table of "Jesus freaks," kids with ideals pushed upon them by their parents and still too young to think for themselves.* His judgment stung when the thought came that he wished he was included. He pictured himself sitting beside the young, blond woman enjoying the exchange of ideas and revelry. And yet, he was not a part of the group, of any group really. After nearly four years in college, he was still trying to find somewhere to fit in.

He sat alone wasting time and fearing the return to his empty apartment, but was unwilling to open one of his books and focus on his studies. When he glanced up, he saw she was smiling at him. She was not unaware of the attention he had given them. He returned the smile, nodded politely, then lowered his head and quickly opened one of his books. For several minutes she continued to openly watch him, disconnecting herself from the table's conversation. She then stood and walked toward him.

"Your book is upside down," she said with a twinkle in her blue eyes.

"I'm having trouble concentrating today," he said.

"Would you like to join us?" she asked, still smiling.

"No," he said, a little too quickly. "I have to study for a test."

"Oh," she answered, sounding disappointed. "Can I join you then?"

63

Dexter found himself falling into her eyes as though he had fallen from a cliff into the azure blue of the oceans' depths.

He seemed to sit without answering for several minutes before he finally nodded and said, "Sure, have a seat. Won't your friends miss you?" he asked, noting that several had looked his way.

"They'll be fine. I won't be gone forever, will I?"

He nodded his head after finding no suitable response.

"What subject?" she asked.

"I'm sorry, what?"

"Your test, what subject?"

He had been caught and he knew it. She knew it, and they knew it together.

He shrugged his broad shoulders and answered, "Sorry, I just made that up. Where are you from?" he asked, trying to redirect the conversation.

"Walla Walla. Have you ever been there?"

"No, but if that's an invite, I'm in."

"Do you think I'm too forward? Too pushy?" she asked.

"No, I think you are beautiful. I mean you are just fine."

She laughed. To Dexter it sounded like the tinkle of a small bell, a light and happy sound.

"I'll take the 'beautiful,' thank you very much," she said, still laughing. "But you can keep the 'just fine.' It makes me feel like you are settling for less than you wanted."

Dexter gave her a puzzled look.

"Haven't you ever ordered a meal that was neither good nor bad, and when the waiter asked about it you said, 'It was just fine'? I try to be a step up from 'just fine' if I can."

He could feel himself turning red with embarrassment, but had no desire to end their conversation. "Are you a freshman?" he asked.

"Does it show?" she asked, looking disappointed. "Do I look like a silly kid?"

He began to say that she looked just fine, but caught himself. "Not really. It's just that I have never noticed you before."

"I've noticed you," she said bluntly. "You are always sitting alone. I couldn't build up the nerve to come over until today."

"I'm kind of a loner, the quiet, mysterious type."

He liked her laugh. In fact he was beginning to like everything about her.

~ ~

He lay there with eyes open, staring at eternity. A crimson rivulet of blood was his only indication of injury. The air bag had done its job well; his torso had been protected from the projecting steering column. A darkening mass under the surface of the smooth skin on his forehead evidenced a hematoma. She looked at him dispassionately, struggling to understand what she was seeing. It seemed only moments before they had shared laughter and the light banter of those drawn to one another.

She struggled to recall his name. Quiet and mysterious, she remembered his self-description but not his name. She leaned toward him and touched his cheek. She wondered if she was hurt, but could feel no pain. Her seat belt restraint had held her firmly and still exerted pressure across her chest. The sounds of emergency workers struggling

65

to gain access, a myriad of flashing lights, and the hushed sounds of men talking in groups of two and three caught her attention.

She wanted to ask questions, to fill the gaps in her memory, and to get reassurance from the EMT who had reached through the broken window to check the young man's vitals. She asked, but he did not answer her directly.

"He's gone," the EMT said, as a statement of fact.

Gone? Gone where? At once the awful realization overcame her, its answer repugnant and unbelievable. *Gone, never to return. Gone to where all who do not know the Savior will some day go.*

~ ~

They sat for several more minutes visiting, working to find common ground on which to build a relationship. She waved to her group of friends as they stood and began to move away from their table. She made no effort to leave or join them, satisfied to share additional moments with Dexter.

"You should join us Wednesday night," she said with sincerity evident in her voice. "We meet at the chapel, sing a little, discuss scripture, pray for a while, and then scrape up what we can to have dinner together."

He nodded as though he understood, but of course he did not. "You're really into this religion thing?"

She looked at him seriously with hurt in her eyes. "This is no religion thing. There are only those who come to salvation through Jesus' sacrifice and those who do not. Religion is a term made up by men to describe something they do not understand."

Dexter felt badly about the way he had phrased it and tried to compensate. "I apologize. My family never had time for church, or religion, or much of anything that didn't make them more money."

As she spoke, he saw sympathy in her eyes. "I guess I am lucky. My family made a point of teaching us what they believed about God. I accepted Jesus when I was ten."

"How could anyone ten years old even know what they want or understand enough about God to decide?"

"Let me try and describe how it was for me."

She started slowly, struggling to describe her feelings from memory. As she began to relive the event, she gained momentum and enthusiasm. The warm memory of giving herself to her Savior brought a flush to her cheeks and tears to her eyes.

Dexter was mesmerized by her beauty, sincerity, honesty, and lack of fear to open herself up to a stranger. He was intrigued by her story and wondered how anyone could believe that strongly in anything they could not see.

When she finished speaking, he said, "Maybe you can tell me more about that later and help me to see things as you see them. We've got plenty of time."

~ ~

Once again the tragic reality returned. The smell of gasoline was overwhelming. She could hear the sounds of men and machines prying at the metal of the crumpled car. His features began to blur, and his body seemed to evaporate before her eyes. Then he was gone.

~ ~

As he looked across the car at her lifeless form, softness blurred the definition of the scene. A warm, golden glow began in her hair, then filled the crushed, metal coffin in which they were trapped. She turned her head toward him and smiled. Peace was written on her beautiful face. Then she was gone.

~ ~

"Can I drive you home for spring break?" Dexter asked. "We can take the new car my folks bought me for Christmas and be there in six hours."

"I don't think so," Gretchen answered. "I think we better stick around and wait until the weather clears over the Cascades. It's a bad road this time of year."

"Come on, live a little," he urged. "I want to meet your folks, and you can tell me more of your life story while we're on the road."

To his eternal loss, they reached "the end of their road" before she was able to tell the rest of her story.

Carpe diem Spiritus Sancti.

Light

"I can't find a pulse," he said, concern evident in his voice as he began compression of the chest. "Get a bag on her."

Linda, tore off the sterile covering from the bag and placed a mask over the victim's mouth and began to squeeze the bulb, forcing air into the lungs.

Bill was senior, both in age and experience, giving him the lead when things became dicey. Linda never questioned his instructions, but sometimes asked for clarification after the crisis had passed. She was a quick learner and possessed a natural aptitude for medicine. At one time she had dreamed of becoming a doctor. That was before the death of her father when the family was still intact. It had not been her grades that had changed her plans, but her mother's need for care and companionship.

When the call came in, Linda immediately knew what she would find. Her parents' address came up on the GPS, automatically directing Bill to the house so familiar to her.

Mae had turned seventy-eight earlier in the month, a fact few outside the family knew. She was a private person who kept the details of her life to herself. Even the twinkle in her blue eyes had disappeared when she had said farewell to the love of her life.

It was Fred, their trusty postman, who had peaked in the window when the doorbell went unanswered. He made the 9-1-1 call when he saw Mae lying on the living room floor.

Bill could feel the frail bones in the aged body crack from time to time as he continued to compress the sternum. "Do you want the paddles?" he asked his partner.

Linda thought, fighting her own emotions, before answering. "We've talked about this many times. She has DNR compression only on the fridge. The last thing she would want is for us to bring her back."

Bill looked at her with tears in his eyes. He then lowered his head. Linda saw his lips move and knew he was praying as he always did for the soul of the patient who was just about to walk into eternity. Somehow Linda knew that her father and mother were already reunited.

"I'm sorry," he said sincerely.

"Thank you," Linda answered, as she began to repack her medical bag. She stood and went to the old rotary phone sitting on the table beside the sofa. She could have used her cell to call the coroner, but chose to honor her mother by using the old one. She remembered that there had to be special modifications made for the old phone to continue to function when everything went digital. Her parents had paid extra for the privilege.

Bill called the station and spoke softly. "Captain said to stay as long as you like. He took us out of service for the rest of the shift."

Linda nodded, appreciating the accommodation. She went into the kitchen and started brewing a pot of coffee.

"Thanks, Bill. It feels right that you are here with me."

Bill was like an older brother to Linda. He and his wife, Megan, had shared holidays, birthdays, funerals, and childbirths with her as naturally as if they were her own family. Linda would turn forty-five this year, the youngest of four children. Bill on the other hand would never see fifty again, with children already out of college. He had graduated with her older brother, Roy, and had been a family fixture as they were growing up. She felt closer to Bill than to Roy now, not only because Roy had moved and made a life that did not include her and her parents, but also because she worked with him each day in life and death situations. Akin, she supposed, to those who served together in the military, police or firemen, their bond was a combination of loyalty, trust, respect and love beyond that which most shared. It was possibly the kind of love that God desires we have for each other when He said, "Love your neighbor as yourself."

~ ~

Lieutenant Tim Murphy, "Murph", estimated that Ahmad had been gone about thirty minutes before he returned and started the old truck. They had only traveled a short distance when Ahmad stopped the vehicle, turned off the headlights, and crawled into the back of the truck with him. Ahmad carried a Russian-made rifle in his hand.

"They were waiting for him," Ahmad said. "When he got to the crossing they turned on a light and stopped him. Now they are beating him, trying to make him tell them our location."

"Who are they?" Murph asked.

"Sunni dogs, killers of women and children," Ahmad spat.

71

"What will you do?"

"Kill them."

"I am sorry I got you into this situation. I am sorry I cannot help," Murph said sincerely.

Ahmad smiled. "No need. You got shot down saving many. It is right that we save you."

The truck started and moved slowly forward. Its lights revealed the road ahead. Ahmad stayed in the back covered by a canvas tarp. Time went by slowly for Murph. He was duct taped to a chair because his weakened body was unable to support itself. He had been blinded by blows to the head doled out by his captors. His rescuers had wrapped him in rags, disguising him as a leper. He was helpless to do anything but pray. Murph could hear and feel movement in the bed of the truck as his friend crawled over the tailgate and rolled into the darkness. As the truck stopped, he heard shouts and threats from both sides of the vehicle. Loud, coarse language, meant for intimidation, assailed his ears as the Sunnis emptied the truck of its passengers and pushed them to the ground. Then the shouting was directed at Murph.

"Unclean," he said, as instructed, then repeated himself again more loudly. He could not see, but felt the beams of bright light trained upon him as his enemies evaluated him.

One attempted to crawl up for a closer look, but was warned back by his jihadist brothers.

"Unclean" he said, again in his best Middle Eastern voice.

Murph recognized three different voices as the men argued over what to do with him.

Unknown to him, a man with an AK-47 had chosen to end the

discussion. The vote had ended with a decision to kill the leper and the other two. The women would be killed later, after being used. Two shots rang out followed by a third a few seconds later. Murph waited, expecting to feel pain in his recently revived body, but he did not.

Ahmad hurried from his hiding spot and greeted his friends. He then turned toward Murph and said, "We were granted safe passage. They have allowed us to pass."

His comments brought laughter from his friends, who stripped the bodies of anything of value and rolled them off the road into the desert sand to be buried.

They were well inside Iraq now, but not safe from Sunnis bent on persecuting their Shiite enemies. Murph heard Ahmad speak into a radio but did not understand what he said or what the reply meant. His eyes had recovered just enough to tell that the sun was rising over the desert. He still could not see well enough to identify objects. The old truck was pulled next to a building and stopped.

Someone untied his chair and lowered it to the ground.

"Where are we?" Murph asked.

"Amarah," Ahmad answered. "We are to wait here before entering the city."

"Are there American forces in the city?"

"I do not know. Are you able to see anything?"

"Light only. How long will the blindness last?"

"I do not know. I was just told it was likely to be temporary."

After Mae's funeral, everyone came over to Linda's house to show their respects. Linda could see the men had gathered in the living room while she and the women cleaned up after the last crumbs of pies and cookies had disappeared.

"Lin, we're kind of thinking barbecue for dinner. How's that sound to you?" Roy asked.

Linda smiled. "We just finished breakfast. You men handle meals as if you were planning the campaigns of a war." Just saying that made her think of her fiancé, Tim. When he was listed as missing in action years ago she filled each day hoping against hope that he would one day return. *He would have loved to be in the room with the guys.*

Her moment of reflection was broken when Roy said, "A man's got to think ahead. No sense waiting until we are hungry to start planning."

"OK," she agreed, "but just how are you going to get enough meat on mom's little gas barbecue to feed the teeming hordes?"

A blank look took the place of eager anticipation on the manly faces until Bill said, "We'll move the gang to my house. We've got a new gas grill, and I still have the old one for backup."

Nods of approval and self-satisfied looks of agreement challenged Linda.

"Good," she said, pretending to give in, "I'll make up a grocery list for you."

~ ~

The phone roused Linda from a sound sleep as she looked toward the clock and attempted to find her cell phone. It was eleven fifteen.

"Did I wake you?" a familiar voice asked.

"No," Linda lied, "I'm just a little tired. It's been a long day."

"This is Joyce. I'm sorry, I didn't realize it was so late. Sometimes I lose track of time."

"It's so nice to hear from you," Linda said. "It's been a long time." She found herself trying to sound gracious, and actually glad to hear from Tim's mother.

"I got a call from someone at the State Department in Washington."

A heavy cloud rested on Linda's chest. "What did they say?"

"Apparently there have been some communications intercepted that referred to Tim by name."

"What kind of communications? Did they find him? Is he alive?"

"They did not say," Joyce answered. "Only that it is very unusual that after all this time his name would appear out of the blue."

Linda's mind was running full tilt. "May I walk down and join you?"

"I'd like that. If you are sure I didn't wake you."

A quick ten-minute walk brought her to the door of Joyce's house.

The short, gray-haired woman opened the door, invited her in, and gave her a long hug. "I've always considered you my daughter," she said.

"And you've always treated me like one," Linda replied.

"Please come in and sit," Joyce invited, motioning to the old sofa. "Would you like some tea?"

"That would be nice."

The room needed paint, new carpet and new draperies, Linda observed. The walls were covered with pictures from an entire generation of Joyce's family. Linda's eyes were drawn to the fireplace mantel where a photograph of Tim dominated. He looked so young and handsome in his uniform, just like the dreams Linda occasionally had of him.

Joyce returned to the room carrying a serving tray with a tea service and two china cups. They sipped their tea silently for a few minutes.

"What do you think I should do?" Joyce asked.

"Do you have a name or phone number to call?" Linda asked.

"No, I didn't think to write the name or number down. Most of the ones I used to call when things like this happened are retired."

"Let's give them a couple of days to try and figure out what the messages are about and see if they call back," Linda suggested. "I suspect that it is the CIA and not the Air Force that is working on it."

"Oh, why do you assume that?" Joyce asked.

"I think they eavesdrop on our enemy's conversations all the time. Somehow the computer must have linked Tim's name to an open case file."

Joyce nodded.

"It's been quite a while since we got together," Linda said. "What have you been doing?"

"Just waiting to go home. When the Lord's ready, I am too. All of my family is already there, except Tim, and he may be too, for all I know."

"Good tea," Linda said, trying to change the subject.

"Earl Grey," Joyce said, proudly. "I think he was an English nobleman or something."

Linda smiled. "The Brits are big tea drinkers. Sounds about right to me."

They talked for a long time, cried a little, prayed for God's will to be done, and then said good night.

Linda crawled back into bed just before two o'clock feeling comforted and at peace. The alarm woke her at a quarter to six. She felt remarkably rested in spite of the scant hours of sleep. Mondays among the eight-to-five crowd were always a downer, but among the firemen it was just another day of the week. The fact that she had only been off for a couple of days made it easy to return to work. She preferred working to staying around an empty house. Flowers and a card were waiting for her from the crew that had been on duty and hadn't been able to attend the funeral.

~ ~

"Dangerous times," Ahmad said matter-of-factly as they headed into the city. "It is often hard to know whom you can trust."

Murph listened to the Iranian without answering.

"Yes, like Jesus said to His disciples, 'brother will deliver up brother up to death, and a father his child.'"

Murph nearly fainted at hearing Jesus' words being quoted from the lips of an Iranian.

"You know Jesus' teachings?" he asked.

"Indeed," he answered, smiling. "Is that not a good part of

77

knowing the One you serve?"

"It is," Murph said. "I assumed you were Muslim."

Ahmad smiled. "One should take care never to assume too much. One can seldom tell the heart by looking at the face."

"So you are a Christian?"

"It is so. Most certainly I am. Was that not apparent as we cared for you?"

"Christians do not have a corner on the market when it comes to being good, kind and generous," Murph answered. "They do have the one true salvation found only in Jesus."

Ahmad nodded his agreement as he pulled the old truck between two ramshackle buildings and turned the motor off. Eager hands unloaded Murphy and carried him inside and out of sight. He sat alone for a time in a small, poorly lit room near the back. He could hear the voices of his newfound friends in the area near the front.

Ahmad joined him. "We have made contact. Someone will be joining us soon. Pray that Jesus will smile down upon us, and they will not be our enemies."

Murph found himself amused at how Ahmad had substituted Jesus' name for Allah in his prayer.

The sound of a vehicle warned them of approaching visitors.

"Remain here and say nothing except what I have told you," Ahmad said, as he left the room.

Murph could hear several voices excitedly speaking Farsi. The door opened and a light panned across the room illuminating him. He waited until movement indicated someone was approaching, then cried out, "Unclean," in his best Farsi dialect. He could make out light and some undefined images and then heard the door being closed. A short time later a vehicle drove away and his friend returned.

"Who were they?" Murph asked. "Are they coming back for me?"

"It is our hope they are friends and someone will certainly be returning for you."

"Someone? If not them, who might that someone be?"

"Possibly your American friends. They carry with them your identification tag."

Murph reached up and noticed that one of his two dog tags had been removed from the chain around his neck. "If not the Americans, who might return?" he asked.

Ahmad smiled. "You are a ripe plum, ready to be picked, my friend. Your enemies have been searching for you and would consider you a prize."

The thought of going back to POW status was unbearable to Murph. *I'd rather be dead*, he thought. "If they come to make me a prisoner again, please kill me," he said, to his friend.

Ahmad smiled with compassion. "If they come to capture you, I will be captured with you as well. Surely I cannot kill my friend. It is not up to us to decide our fates. We must place our lives in God's hands."

~ ~

Linda was emotionally and physically exhausted from a long day at work and fell asleep as soon as her head hit the pillow. She was awakened twelve hours later by a phone call.

"Linda, dear, is that you?"

"Yes, Joyce, I'm here," Linda answered, sweeping the cobwebs out of her head.

"They called me back. There is reason to believe Tim may have survived," she said happily. "They don't have details yet, but one of the locals gave his dog tag to the U.S. Embassy saying he was alive."

Linda nearly collapsed as she tried to get out of bed. She struggled to breathe as the implications overwhelmed her. She had so many questions and so few answers. How cruel it would be if it was just another false report.

"Are you still there, dear?" Joyce said.

"Yes, Joyce, I'm just struggling to believe that it could be possible."

"I know. I've tried not to get my hopes up, but I can't help it."

"Have you eaten?" Linda asked.

"No," Joyce admitted, "I had a bite this morning and I don't usually eat lunch. It's no fun to eat alone."

"Let's get something to eat. It'll be my treat. When should I pick you up?" "Whenever you are ready, dear. I'll be looking for you."

~ ~

Murph could hear the sound of several vehicles. Each one seemed to be approaching the building from a different direction. There were loud noises as the outside doors burst open, and men shouted as they entered. It was a "shock and awe" approach. The noise and bluster was supposed to overwhelm the enemy's senses, making their resistance seem futile. He could also make out vague outlines of objects around him in the room. *Praise God*, he said silently, *my eyesight is returning.*

The two squads had rightfully been wary of an invitation to recover one of their own that had been missing for years. It had smelled like a trap, which required caution, but also mandated investigation. Thankfully for everyone involved, their mission was legitimate and ended without casualty.

The first American voice he heard was someone with a thick Texas drawl. "Lieu-ten-ant Murphy, we have come to take you home," the sergeant said. He removed the duct tape that had held Murph in the chair. The squads formed two lines, stood at attention, and saluted Murph as he was carried toward the waiting vehicles.

Murph began to cry. Tears of joy and relief ran down his cheeks as he sobbed unashamedly. In the vacant warehouse, the brave Shiite group who had rescued him and brought him to safety assembled to say their farewells.

He was helped into the seat of the Humvee by Ahmad. Murph took the chain with its remaining dog tag from his neck and placed it on his friend.

"Please, when you are safe, contact the U.S. Embassy. I'll leave instruction with them as to how you may contact me. I will never forget any of you. Sergeant, is there a way you could take a picture of my friends for me?" Murph said, as he motioned at the Iranians standing nearby.

"Certainly, sir," he said. He pulled out his cell phone and started taking pictures.

"That's a pretty small camera, Sergeant," Murph observed. "Are you sure it will take quality pictures?"

"It's my cell phone, sir," he answered. "You've been away for a while. It takes very good digital pictures that can be transmitted via satellite to anywhere in the world. When you are ready, we can set you up online and you can see and talk to your family back home."

"We'll be able to see and hear each other?" Murph asked. "My cell phone was a Motorola that I carried around in a bag the size of a shaving kit and had a very limited range."

~ ~

Linda pulled to the curb and saw Joyce coming out the front door. Joyce smiled but Linda could tell she had been crying.

"They called. He's been rescued and is on his way to the hospital. They said that within a day or so we'll be able to talk with him," Joyce said.

Linda turned off the ignition. For several moments no one spoke, as they silently thanked God.

At the café they took a booth near the back.

"Just tea for now," Linda said, speaking for both of them. "We'll hold onto the menus for later."

"Why did he go to the hospital? Was he hurt?" Linda said, not necessarily to anyone. "Do we even dare to believe it is true?" Just then Linda was reminded of a chorus she had sung in church last Sunday. *Let faith arise. God is on our side. The battles won. God is with us. He is for us. Faithful is our God.*

They each ordered a bowl of soup and a club sandwich while they shared their hearts.

"They said that if I had a computer link they could transmit directly to me by satellite. Do you know what that means?" Joyce asked.

"They can uplink both video and audio and put it on your computer so you can hear and see each other."

"I don't have a computer anymore. It stopped working so I got rid of it."

"We can use mine," Linda said.

"I kind of feel like Simeon who was allowed to live until the Savior was born. I have prayed for years that he would be alive and that I might live to see him again."

83

Linda nodded and wondered what the future held for them. Was he badly hurt? Would they still feel what they once had felt for each other? If he had been alive all this time, where had he been and why had he not contacted them? Her joy was disturbed by her questioning nature.

~ ~

Murph was taken to the infirmary where he was debriefed and then underwent initial physical and psychological tests. His eyesight continued to improve as Ahmad had suggested. The consensus of the doctors was that his initial injuries had healed long ago, but during the many years of captivity many of his muscles had atrophied to the point of uselessness. The doctors prescribed a treatment regimen that included therapies specifically designed for each muscle and muscle group.

He was taken to a private office where a computer had been linked to Linda's. He was shown how the system worked, and they sent her a message to contact them. That day when she returned home from work, she saw the message.

"Joyce," Linda said, "they tried to contact us while I was at work. I just emailed them to tell them we will be waiting for their reply. Can you come over?"

"I'm on my way," Joyce said excitedly.

They sat together, almost counting the seconds. They chatted for nearly an hour before the computer came to life.

The Skype program allowed them to communicate by video call. A younger version of Joyce's husband was looking right at them.

With tears running down his cheeks, he spoke softly and

carefully to their images on the screen. "Linda, Mom, this is Murph, Tim Murphy. I can see you. Can you see me?"

"Yes, Tim, we can see you," Linda said.

"It's been so long. It's so good to see you."

"They said you'd been taken to the hospital. We've been so worried. Are you hurt?" Linda asked.

"They say that time and therapy will get everything working again," Tim answered.

"Were you wounded, son?" Joyce asked. "Were you captured?"

"I was badly wounded when my plane was shot down, and held as an unreported prisoner of war for a long time. I was recently rescued by friendly forces."

As they talked, asked and answered questions, they became more and more comfortable with the computer link. Finally it felt just as if they were in the same room with the screen disappearing from consciousness. Tim shared the details of his plane being shot down, his captivity, rescue, and the events of the last forty-eight hours.

Linda held up her hand to the webcam, showing her engagement ring. "I've about worn this out waiting for the second one," she joked. "Are we still on?" It was the first time in years she felt like laughing about being a fiancée.

Tim became serious. "So the answer is still yes?"

"Too late to back out now. I've told all the guys within a hundred miles that I'm already taken."

It was three hours later when they finally ended the conversation. They promised to repeat it daily until he returned.

"Why don't you consider moving in with me for a while?" Linda asked Joyce. "That way one of us will always be here when Tim calls."

"Are you sure?" Joyce asked tentatively. "I don't want to trouble you."

"It's no trouble. In fact, I will enjoy the company. It's been awfully quiet since Mom passed."

~ ~

By the end of the second week Murphy could stand for short periods with help. He also had full use of his arms. The regimen included physical therapy twice a day, counseling, and long hours at the computer trying to piece together the history of the world. He thought of the young men around him as his peers. They thought of him as their father. He was having difficulty adapting to all the changes that had taken place while he was in captivity.

He spent hours each day talking with Linda and his mother, trying desperately to catch up on the past before looking forward to the future. After ten more days he was walking short distances without help, but tired easily. It was then that command began talking about sending him home. Frightened was how his counselor described it: afraid of the expectations of others, afraid of failure, uncertain of what he would do or how he would be accepted. He began long sessions with the chaplain in an attempt to regain his faith, but felt little progress.

One day the chaplain asked him, "What single thing have you learned from all of this?"

"What do you mean?"

"I mean exactly what I said," he answered roughly. "Think about it before you give me an answer."

Murph did not meet with the chaplain for two days, but the question was never far from his mind. He struggled, prayed, reasoned and deliberated on the question.

"That God is in control of everything. We live and exist by His grace," Murph said triumphantly.

"Amen," the chaplain said with a smile. "With that being said, what do you fear? What should you fear?"

"I fear what others will think of me, if I can please them, and if I can make a life for myself," he answered, honestly. "And I am afraid of those same kinds of things with God: What will God think of me? Will I be able to please Him? Have I, or will I ever, be able to meet His expectations?"

"We'll talk about other people in a minute. But let's deal with your fears about God first. You and I are clear about the fact that you have accepted God's offer of forgiveness, right?"

"Of course."

"So based upon Jesus' sacrifice for sin, God has accepted you into His family and removed the guilt of your sin. He has promised his children that He will never leave nor forsake them, and He will never remove His love from them. That should take care of the whole issue of being afraid of what God thinks about you. Now, did you become a part of His family by living up to His standards or by Christ's sacrifice?"

"Wow! I haven't really given that enough thought. You're right. It wasn't based on my good behavior, but on what Jesus did for me."

"So being afraid of your inability to meet His expectations isn't really an issue either, is it?"

"I get it. It's not about me being good enough for God. It's about being accepted into His family."

"I think that you will find that the people waiting for you will be just as forgiving and supportive as God. Most of them can't wait to welcome you back home. Now, are you ready to go home and marry the girl that has been waiting for you all of these years?"

"Yes, sir, I am," Murph said, with tears in his eyes and a smile on his face.

~ ~

After nearly thirteen hours in the air, he finally arrived. He stepped off the plane to a gathering of friendly faces, most of whom he did not even know. A local school band played, the Veterans of Foreign Wars was represented, and the American flag was in the hands of innumerable school-age children who had come to see the local hero. The mayor, city councilmen, a congressman, and the new commander of his wing awaited him on the tarmac. His eyes searched for Linda and his mother in the crowd. Klieg lights on mobile pedestals illuminated the area for the "newsies" standing about with microphones in hand. On either side of the red carpet runner stood eight men in full dress uniform with their hands frozen in a salute.

When the commander stepped forward, Murph raised his right hand in salute.

The band was silenced as the commander spoke into the microphone. "Welcome home Lieutenant Murphy. We have all waited a long time to say those words."

Linda and his mother came running from the crowd and were gathered up in his arms.

Autonomous

Was it more than society's repetitive worship of individualism, or was it pride, or some more insidious force that caused him to believe that he held the power over his own destiny? He could quote all the maxims, which gave glory to man and his accomplishment at the cost of minimizing God. By the sweat of his brow, pulled up by his boot straps, discipline, hard work, focus, self-made man, determination, work ethic, ambition, foresight, and self-sacrifice were a few of the words used to glorify man's efforts toward accomplishment.

What he had that others lacked was first, a gifting from God and second, the desire to utilize it. What he lacked was the recognition of the real source of the gift. Like many, if not most, he was easily able to accept good fortune and attribute it to himself. Carl had the advantage of intelligence, a family blessed with prosperity, good health, and better than average appearance. He was both powerful and ruthless.

Mr. Carlton Williams, CEO and tyrant, lived to personally exert his will and demonstrate his considerable power to his subordinates. A man three times divorced, richer than Solomon, and smarter too, if you would believe his own press releases, Carl was at the top of his game. At thirty, he was a rising star to others who would come longing to eat crumbs from his table. Nearly universally respected for his business acumen, he was also hated and feared by competitors and employees alike. His only allies were others like him who used each other for personal gain.

Words like shark, powerbroker, piranha, and cut throat were apt descriptions of the man and the attitude he personified. Someone once asked him, "How much is enough?" referring to his personal wealth. He replied with a sneer, "There isn't ever enough."

At age twelve he would have been described as an average boy from an average family. He lived with his parents, attended public school, and did what most young men do. By age fourteen his grandmother had died, leaving his family a vast fortune. By year's end they had sold her mansion and built a larger one with her money. The family fell easily into the life that great wealth provided and learned quickly that with enough money nearly anything was possible.

He was in college when his parents died. They were in their private jet when it crashed into the sea. With the help of tutors he put his education on the fast track, earning a master of business administration in just over four years. He hired the best minds that money could buy, picked their brains, and sent them down the road. As his knowledge grew so did his wealth. His name became familiar to others who possessed power and money.

But to Carl it was not enough. Inside, the fear of poverty gnawed at him like a cur dog eating scraps in an alley. With each victory came the fear of future defeat. He married, not for love, but from a need to look married. In the end, even his wealth could not provide them with happiness, and each wife left the mansion as they came, but somewhat wiser after rereading their prenuptial agreement. It was once said that the wealthy looked down on the rich the way billionaires looked down on millionaires. That made perfect sense to Carl.

In some ways Carl was a personal dichotomy, with one part of him happy to spend his wealth lavishly, seeking notice and approval, and the other frugal, secretly looking for ways to hoard his fortune. He was a voracious reader with an almost photographic memory, which gave him an edge in business. He took full advantage of men who diminished their skills with the use of drugs and alcohol. Carl also had a keen interest in history, believing that men could learn from the past and use it to direct their own futures. That is how Carl came to be acquainted with the Bible. He saw it not as a religious work, or some great instruction manual written as a guide to right living, but as an accurate account of past history. He gave little thought to the spiritual side, but developed a keen interest in what worked and what had not worked for kings and leaders from the past. He was particularly enamored with King Solomon because of his wealth and achievements.

Carl was not an evil man, but a man seemingly without conscience in respect to his business dealings. He clearly saw Solomon's wisdom concerning the two women who both claimed the same child, but missed the point concerning the humanity that pointed him to the true mother. Carl could neither be described as happy nor unhappy, but more or less ambivalent about life in general. He worked fifteen- to twenty-hour days, leaving little time to consider the condition of his life. His goals, if he had any, were not quantified or measured in a way that would give either satisfaction or remorse.

As the years went by, his amassed fortunes became nearly

incalculable. He became reclusive and withdrew from the societal limelight. At age forty-two he was diagnosed with ALS. After literally scouring the world and spending fortunes searching for a cure, he returned home, resigning himself to suffer and die early in life.

Carl knew how to make money, had learned how to spend money, but lacked the knowledge of the true value of money until one morning when the butler brought his mail to him. It was Carl's practice to peruse every piece of mail personally before applying sticky notes with instructions to his subordinates about what needed to be done. He was a very detailed, hands-on leader. A single piece of mail caught his eye, an envelope apparently addressed by a shaky hand with a cheap handwritten thank you card inside. It simply said, "Thank you. Your generosity allowed me to purchase food and medicine this month. Love, Carla Gifford."

He was surprised and intrigued by the note as he set it aside. He knew that his many corporations had gained tax breaks by donating to a vast number of worthy causes. He also knew that he was personally insulated from them in order to prevent unwanted solicitation. Yet somehow this Carla Gifford person had been persistent and diligent enough to pick the lock and find out not only where the money came from, but also to obtain his personal mailing address. For the first time in years he enjoyed an emotional moment - or several of them if the truth were known. The first was fear; fear that someone could gain access to his personal information. He then felt curiosity about what motivated them to do so. And finally, he wondered what they hoped to gain.

"James, please get the Drake agency on the phone for me," he said, to his butler.

The aged butler nodded and answered his intention to do so right away.

"Drake Investigations," came the deadpan greeting on the phone. "How may I direct your call?"

"Put John on. Tell him Carl Williams is calling," he ordered.

"Right away, Mr. Williams." The receptionist's voice had taken on a warmer tone as she recognized the significant caller.

"John," Carl said without preamble, "I need you to personally handle something for me right away."

John Drake was not small potatoes himself. He founded and ran the largest security agency in the world. Foreign leaders, the CIA, and powerful magnates would contact the agency when they had covert or clandestine missions that needed to be handled confidentially.

It had been many years since John had been a gumshoe, freelance private investigator. He no longer handled anything personally. He was intrigued by the tone of Carl's voice.

"Of course, Carl, right away. I'll send my best man right over."

"No, John," Carl said with conviction, "I want you personally to look into a matter for me."

Under other circumstances John would have laughed and provided an excuse to placate a good client. But something in Carl's tone warned him that a twenty million dollar account hung in the balance.

"As you wish, Carl. I may be a little rusty; I haven't done any legwork in ten years."

Carl's tone became friendlier. "I am sure you can handle it. Just like riding a bicycle, isn't it?"

John nearly laughed at the analogy. He could not picture Carl

Williams as ever being a child, or much less ever having ridden a bicycle. "I'll be there within the hour."

John Drake was as close to a friend as Carl had ever known, and yet they were simply business associates of long standing. He was trusted by necessity to be privy to many things that only Carl knew because of John's need to get an overall view and provide an impenetrable blanket of security for Carl's diversified worldwide holdings. When he entered the code at the gate and was permitted entry, his eyes surveyed the vast estate making mental note of the unseen eyes and ears that had been securely installed by his company. *It would be quite a challenge for even the best-trained assault forces to penetrate this fortress*, he thought. He might suggest it to his friend in the CIA as an advanced training exercise for some future time.

"Morning, Carl," John said, sticking out his hand to the man seated behind the desk. "How are you holding up?"

In a manner totally out of character, Carl smiled and said, "I'm dying, but not today."

John had known of the disease for over a year. Only recently had the business community also became aware. "We all are," he answered, attempting to keep the moment light. "It's just a matter of when."

Carl nodded, then slid the woman's card across the table. "I want to know all about this person," he said. "Keep it low key and private. I don't want her or anyone else to know you're snooping around."

John looked over the card and envelope carefully and stuck them in his brief case. "I'll have a look and get back to you this evening."

"Thank you, John," Carl said uncharacteristically.

Carl seldom thanked anyone for anything, feeling that paying their fee was thanks enough.

~ ~

John was a little disappointed when he looked in the phone directory and found a listing for Carla Gifford at the same address listed on the envelope. As he drove slowly by the small house, he noted that although the neighborhood was probably built in the 40s or 50s, nearly all of the homes seemed well kept. He parked at the corner of the adjacent block and attached the patch cord from his cell phone to a mini-recorder before dialing.

"Mrs. Gifford, Mrs. Carla Gifford?" John asked, when she answered her phone.

"Yes, this is Carla Gifford. Who is this?"

"My name is John. I am a friend of Mr. Carl Williams. He asked if I would stop and visit with you if it is convenient."

"I am not sure I know a Carl Williams," she answered. "Perhaps you have the wrong Carla Gifford."

John had not wanted to mention the card until he had gotten inside and had a look around, but she had forced his hand. "You sent him a nice thank you card."

She tried to remember which particular card had gone to what person. "Oh, yes, I remember now. I had a difficult time getting his mailing address."

"I'm just a short distance away," John said. "He asked me to stop and thank you personally. May I stop by?"

"Yes, of course, but it is really not necessary. It was he that did me the great service."

"I'll stop just for a minute since I'm here. Then I can tell him that we met."

John felt he should kill a few minutes so he drove down the street a few blocks and stopped at a Handi-Mart. He went inside and bought a small spray of cut flowers, a box of sugar cookies, and a quart of chocolate ice cream.

The doorbell had a piece of tape over it, indicating it was out of service, so he knocked and waited under the stoop. When the door opened, John found himself looking into the pale-blue eyes of a woman he judged to be in her eighties.

"Mrs. Gifford?" he said, smiling. "I'm John Drake. We just spoke."

She looked him over critically until her eyes spied the flowers.

96

"Oh my, asters and zinnias and such beautiful colors. Please come right in."

John handed her the flowers and watched her old face come alive.

"These are beautiful," she said, and then laughed. "I haven't had a man bring me flowers since Albert passed. Let me put these in a vase."

When she went to the kitchen to take care of the flowers, John used his cell phone to shoot a couple dozen pictures of her and her home.

They spent nearly an hour visiting and sharing ice cream and cookies.

"You mentioned having a hard time getting Mr. Williams' address. How did you get it?"

She smiled coyly. "I'm persistent. I just kept asking questions and working my way up the ladder until I finally tired them out. I told them I wouldn't take no for an answer."

By the time John left the smiling widow, he had decided not to bill Carl for the time. He couldn't remember the last time he'd enjoyed his work as much. "Make a note to get out of the office more," he said to himself.

~ ~

"Carl, John here. I have my report for you, but I'd like to deliver it personally if you don't mind."

"Is it urgent? I'm feeling the need for some rest."

"No, things are fine. I'll come by late tomorrow morning."

"Yes, that will be fine," Carl said.

The clock in the car read ten fifteen when John passed through the secure gate and parked under the overhang of the grand entry. He carried his briefcase, which held a full, official, written report, a dozen pictures that awaited Carl's inspection, and an invoice marked "no charge."

John had never seen Carl in a wheelchair before, but this morning he was pushed up to the table in the sunroom with a shawl around his shoulders, awaiting the arrival of his guest.

"Held up breakfast for you," Carl said matter-of-factly, motioning to a seat beside him. "Join me."

John sat at the table and accepted the coffee James placed before him. "Thank you, James," he said, smiling at the tall, colored man who seemed a throwback from the Civil War days.

James nodded and became part of the background scenery.

"What did you find?" Carl asked, sorting through his fruit cup.

John set the report on the table between them and said, "Just what I'd hoped to find. A lonely, little, widow lady who lives in the house her husband bought right after he returned from the war. A woman who is still savvy enough to outsmart your gatekeepers one at a time until she worked her way up to where someone gave up and gave her your name and address."

Carl eyed him suspiciously.

"I see her with no motive other than the good manners she was taught as a child to say thank you when someone has done something nice for you."

"If she could get my address, others can too," Carl said.

"If it were that easy, someone with designs on your money

would have done it long ago. I think it was by God's design that the right set of circumstances came together."

"Why, John, I didn't know you were a religious man."

John felt himself rise to the bait but resisted the challenge to debate with the man. "I am not religious, as you refer to it," John answered quietly. "I am a Christian, saved by the blood of Jesus."

"How are the two different?" Carl asked, sounding perplexed.

John smiled. "Religion is what man thinks God wants. Salvation is what God knows man needs. Tell me, Carl, what is the one thing you want that you can't buy?"

"My health," Carl answered without thought.

"And, if you could buy it, what price would you be willing to pay?"

"Anything, everything. I'd give it all to be healthy and start over."

"And then what? After you regained your health, you'd still die someday wouldn't you?"

"What's your point?" Carl said testily.

"My point, the point that God wants us to consider, is that every living creature He has created will someday die, rich or poor, no exceptions. You'll die, I'll die, and Carla Gifford will die. But the difference is that she and I will live with God for all eternity."

John took an envelope from his briefcase, opened it, and took out several photos of the old woman and her home. He handed them to Carl.

"She's eighty-eight years old, may not see eighty-nine, struggles with diabetes and a failing heart, but I can tell you for a fact that she wouldn't trade places with you," John said with conviction.

"Did she ask you for anything? Did she act like she expected us to continue to help her out financially?"

"Nope, not a thing. As a matter-of-fact, she sent a gift along and asked that I give it to you."

John placed a New King James leather-bound Bible on the table. On its cover was engraved in gold leaf, "Carl Williams."

"I have Bibles," Carl said smugly.

"Not one that an old woman bought with her Social Security check and took the time to have engraved, I'll wager."

"You really care about her, don't you?"

John nodded. "Yes, and all the more now that I know her."

Carl looked at him quizzically. "What is that supposed to mean?"

"It means that we who have committed our hearts to Jesus are commanded to love one another as He loves us," John said, trying to keep it simple. "Because He loves all of His creation, we are called to do the same."

Carl was genuinely interested. "Let me get this straight. You are supposed to love me and others like me even though you have never met them? How about the part that says to love your enemies? How could anyone do that?"

John found himself in the presence of a highly intelligent man who might as well have been in the first grade in respect to his spirituality. So he began with the basics.

"The word love in ancient languages had more than one meaning, as it does today here in America. For example, you love your children differently than your aunt, your wife in a way that you can't love your parents, your friends and neighbors, and yes, even your enemies. God loves us and none are worthy of that love. I can love others in that same way with no strings attached. No one has to earn my love – it is free. Love can mean to care about someone's welfare, in respect to their health and general well-being. Or it can mean a closer and more intimate bond. Carla Gifford cares about your physical well-being, but even more, she cares about your spiritual condition."

James leaned toward his employer and spoke to him quietly.

"Let them wait," Carl said. "Tell them that I am presently unavailable."

James nodded and left the room.

John started to stand, but Carl waived him back to his seat. "Let them wait a few minutes. They're working on my dime. Can I trust you to answer me honestly if I ask you a question?"

"Always."

"Do you love me? Do you really care about me as a person, about my health, if I live or die? Or is it about the considerable business I send your way?" Carl asked.

John considered the question momentarily before answering. "I love you first and foremost because you are God's creation. I care about you because He cares about you and instructs me to care in the same way. I have a deep and personal concern for your spiritual health as well as your physical health. By the way, I love James in the same way, and he holds no profit motive for me."

"Thank you for your report," Carl said in a tone of dismissal. "I'll get back to you if I need more."

John stood and left the room without speaking.

That went well, John thought as he pulled his BMW through the gate and onto the highway. He had a broad smile on his lips. He prayed silently as he drove back to his office. *God, open the eyes of the blind and the ears of the deaf. Call their hearts to you as those who walk in darkness and ignorance.* He had prayed this same prayer many times without a particular person in mind.

~ ~

"A year, maybe less," Carl said, into the phone. "The doctors don't really know."

It had been two months since John had spoken with Carl.

"I'm sorry," John said softly.

"I have a big project for you to work on personally. Will you join me this evening for dinner so that we may discuss the details?"

John noted it had been a request with no veiled underlying threat. He squirmed in his seat trying to find a way to say what needed to be said. "I'm afraid I can't tonight. It's my anniversary, and I have a commitment to my wife."

"How many years?" Carl asked.

"Twenty-two," John answered proudly.

"Have they been happy?"

"Mostly," John answered, remembering some of the rough spots.

"I could never get the hang of it," Carl said wistfully. "I tried but failed all three times."

"I imagine it is harder for a man in your position."

"How so?"

"The way the world is, and the way we are, money complicates things. Where it makes things easier in some ways, it makes them more difficult in others."

"Truer words," Carl said, quoting someone no one remembered. "I wonder if I were to give your wife a personal invitation, if she might allow me to provide your anniversary dinner. I promise not to talk business."

John reflected on the offer, considered their dinner plans, and said, "Let me visit with her and tell her to expect your call. I'll leave it up to her to make the decision."

"Agreed," Carl said.

"Hi Cindy," John said, as she picked up the phone. "I've got a favor to ask. You remember me talking about Carl Williams. He asked permission to call you and invite us to his home for dinner tonight."

"But," she began.

"I know, I told him it was our anniversary, but he insisted on calling anyway," John said.

"So you want me to say yes to him? Is that the favor?"

"No, I would never ask you to do that. The favor is just for you to take his call. I'll back any decision you make."

"But he's a big client isn't he, and you'd like it if we accommodate him," she said with sarcasm evident in her voice.

"I already told him no," John said. "If you don't want to talk with him, just say so and I'll call him back. I am not pressuring you to do anything."

"Okay," she said, sounding unconvinced. "I'll listen to what he has to say."

~ ~

"Mrs. Drake, I'm Carl Williams. I asked John if I may call and extend a dinner invitation to you this evening. I understand that this is a special day for you, and I hope that I might make it even more special."

Smooth, Cindy thought, *this guy is smooth.*

"John seems bent on teaching me how to love others, and I just thought that I might be privileged to see how love really looks."

He let his words hang in the air until she broke the silence.

"What time would you like us to come?" she asked.

"Whatever time is convenient for you. But give us time to enjoy the evening together before we dine."

When Cindy hung up the phone, she was actually looking forward to the evening in spite of her previous reservations.

"John, I called Bitthoff's and canceled our dinner reservations. Mr. Williams is expecting us around six. Is that all right?"

"If you are sure," John answered. "If we don't have a good time we'll hit Bitthoff's tomorrow night."

"What did you tell him about us?" she asked curiously. "He said something strange about you teaching him how to love."

"I'm afraid he's struggling with end-of-life issues and doesn't know Jesus. I don't think he's ever loved anyone except maybe his parents. His gods have always been money, status, success and prestige."

"I remember when you were just like him," Cindy said.

"So do I," John admitted. "There but for the grace of God."

~ ~

It was three minutes before six when James opened the door and greeted John and Cindy. As he took their coats, they could hear music playing in another part of the house. As they entered the dining room, Cindy surmised that it could have seated a hundred. At the far end of the room a six-piece stringed orchestra was playing softly. As they approached the table, several dozen were already seated, including their host and Carla Gifford. Servers in tuxedos, with white gloves, attended to the needs of the guests at the table.

When Carl rose from his wheelchair and signaled, the music stopped. He held his wine glass high and said, "May I propose a toast to John and Cindy Drake, who have allowed us to share in their special day?"

The assembly arose and turned toward them. All smiled and held their glasses high.

After dinner had been served and dessert consumed, the music took on a more active tempo. The guests were encouraged to join John and Cindy on the dance floor. John took note that most of the guests were poorly dressed and had long ago qualified for AARP membership. John asked and received Cindy's permission to ask Carla for a dance.

Later in the evening John said to Carl, "I am curious about your additional guests. They are hardly the ones I would have expected."

Carl smiled. "I have spent the last several weeks reading the gift that Mrs. Gifford so generously gave. I came upon Jesus' words in Matthew chapter 25, verses 35 through 40, which she has helped me to understand. I was able, with her help, to invite some less fortunate than us to share in your celebration."

105

Remembering the Scripture, *When I was hungry ... when I was thirsty ...*, John understood correctly that the guests were from homeless shelters. He started to ask, but was waived off by his host.

"I promised that we'd not talk business," Carl said. "There will be time enough tomorrow to talk about what I have in mind."

As the evening came to an end and a chartered bus pulled up to the mansion, Carla leaned toward John, winked, and said, "Ask him about salvation."

As it turned out Carla had helped Carl find the peace he had searched for his entire life. Carl set up a foundation to administer his fortunes upon his death. It was designed to provide for the aged, widowed, homeless and infirmed. Beyond that, it also provided training and education for those able to work, and halfway houses across the nation for those searching for a better life. Carl hoped they could find it, as he did, by giving their lives to God.

Courageous

He was amazed at how often people misread his motivations. He knew that some thought of him as courageous, while others thought he was just plain stupid. Those who knew him well understood that there was a mixed bag of emotions. Fear and anger were somewhat controlled by integrity. Though much like a geyser, the pressure was building, looking for release.

~ ~

"Breaker 1-9. J.J. is that you? Come back."

"James Jonathan Reynolds at your service, Rooster. I thought I heard your voice on the chatter box. What are you doing in this neck of the woods?" J.J. asked.

"I've got a load out of Seattle headed for The Peg. I thought you were hauling for Timberland Express."

"I was, but they kept changing my route and mixing it with container loads. The wife got tired of never knowing when I might get home."

"Yeah, this is a tough job for a family man. It's better to be fancy free like me," Rooster crowed.

"I am so sick of this weather. I've been fighting it all day, and it doesn't look like it'll get any better where I'm going," J.J. complained.

"I think you're about to get shut down. I've been hearing some squawk about I-94 being locked down at Beach."

"Don't tell me that. I can't afford any downtime."

"If the reports are correct, you won't have a choice. Let me check and get back at ya," Rooster suggested.

"Copy."

~ ~

"Breaker, Breaker 10-45. Anyone out there able to give me a 10-13 for I-94 North Dakota? The Rooster over."

"Rooster, this is Billy Big Rig. Where you headed? Over."

"I'm rolling out of Glendive headed east for The Peg."

"I've got bad news for you. I just passed Beach and they were shutting 94 down. This blizzard is really rollin' through the badlands. You're going to have to wait this one out."

"Copy that. Thanks for shuttin' me down," Rooster complained.

"Hey, Bubba, don't blame me. You can give that one to the NoDak Polar Bear."

"I know. Preesh-y-a-dit," Rooster said apologetically.

"10-4. Billy Big Rig out."

~ ~

"Breaker 1-9. J.J., you got your ears on? Come back," Rooster called out.

"What'd ya hear, Rooster?" J.J. asked.

"Boulevard 94 is closed at Beach. We're down for the count. What's your 20?"

"I just passed yardstick 220."

"Looks like we are going to be held up in Wibaux. How about joining me for a confab at the Shamrock?" Rooster suggested.

"Copy. Be there in 30. Over," J.J. replied.

"I'll be waitin' on you. The Rooster is down 'n out."

~ ~

When Rooster pulled into the Shamrock he saw J.J.'s rig parked out back. He smiled as he thought of how many times they had run into each other on the road. Their friendship went way back to their childhood days. Despite the fact that they were both on the road, they had somehow managed to keep in touch. He couldn't wait to hear the latest account of J.J.'s adventures. As he walked in and looked around, he could see the mixture of ranchers and truckers that were a part of the daily mix at the Shamrock. It wasn't hard to find J.J. with his raggedy old Vikings hat. Rooster couldn't believe that he still wore that old thing, or that he could stay with a team that had made it to the big dance four times and couldn't post a single win.

"What's up with the big hero? I've been hearing some chatter about you pulling off a Superman feat back up in Idaho. They're saying that some trucker pulled a woman out of a forty-six-car pileup on 84 near Boise. The chatter is that it was Jimmy John," Rooster said, right off baiting J.J. for the inside story.

"Hey, leave the redneck radio in the rig," J.J. said, trying to change the topic.

The waitress came over and asked if they would like some coffee. Rooster nodded and flirted a little. She responded with a knowing smile and turned to help someone at another table.

"Just tell me straight, are you the Jimmy John everyone is talking about?"

"Yeah, I was there. It was a bloody mess. There was just a little fog and things were moving along pretty well. All of a sudden the deep fog rolled in," J.J. recalled. "They said that there were a couple of cars that had sideswiped each other and one of them was hit by a logging truck. That is when all hell broke loose. The road was slick and there was no escapin'. I heard it before I saw it. All that I could see through the fog was people sitting in their cars getting banged around like bumper cars at a fair. It was unbelievable."

"So, get to the good stuff. You know, the part where you just had to be the hero," Rooster demanded.

"Why do you always do that? As long as I've known you, you want to make something into something it's not. You know I have no desire to be a hero," J.J. said with disgust apparent in his voice and on his face.

"Oh really? You forget who you are talking to. I'm not some rookie reporter. I'm your friend. I know every stupid and heroic thing you've ever done, including the ones no one else will ever hear about."

"Yeah right. Name one time that I ever gave you the impression that I wanted to be a hero."

"Are you kidding? It's been in your genes since the day you were born."

"OK, name one time, just one time, buddy."

Rooster went through his mental files of their childhood days. "OK, how about the time we went fishing at Lake of the Woods? Same kind of stupid story like the one you just came through. Remember? We were caught in a peat fire fog on the way to the lake. The fog was so dense that we couldn't even see the hood ornament on the Chrysler. You hung your head out the window looking at the yellow lines on the road. Did you really think you were helping the driver by watching those lines?"

"I will never forget that day. We nearly got ourselves killed twice. That was a twofer. We were rolling along at about five miles an hour and all of a sudden there was this incredible crashing sound all around us. I heard a hubcap roll right past my open window. I was expecting that we would be in a pileup that day. I can't believe that we rolled through that without seeing a thing. It was just like those NASCAR guys who fly through a wreck on the track and can't see a thing, but they just blast through it at full speed," J.J. said.

"Yeah, everyone in the car had this panicked look on their face…everyone but you. No kidding, you looked excited like you had just ridden the biggest rollercoaster at the fair. I couldn't believe how calmly you walked through that like it was no big deal." Rooster recalled.

"OK, so you've proven that I was stupid as a kid, but that's nothing heroic."

"Really? And how about later that day when we finally made it to Lake of the Woods? The waves were three to four feet and you still wanted to go out fishing. Your dad knew that we would get skunked and that it wasn't worth the risk. But no, you still wanted to go."

"Hey, that wasn't my call. It wasn't my boat."

"That was quite a day. When the wind came up I remember being in the middle of that lake in that twenty-foot cabin cruiser, and the debate about trying to make it back to the dock against the ten-foot waves, or moving with the waves and trying to make it to Warroad. I've never seen adult men so afraid in my entire life. Do you remember Gordon putting on two life jackets? He was so big that he could barely make one life jacket fit. He looked like Santa Claus trying to fit into a midget's coat. Do you remember what he said when they asked him why he was trying to put on two life jackets?" Rooster asked.

112

"Uff da, that was something that is pretty hard to forget. 'There's a lot of Gordie here, ya know.'" J.J. said, with a whimsical smile.

"And where were you five minutes later? You were down at the front of the boat measuring how far each wave came on the lower window. You were having the time of your life. There was not an ounce of fear in your eyes."

"Alright, you've made it clear that I was a dumb kid, and you were there as a witness. So what does that prove?"

"That proves that I know you, and know what I'm talking about when I say that you are fearless and heroic."

The waitress stepped over from an adjacent table. "Sorry, I didn't mean to be eavesdropping on you guys, but I couldn't help but hear the yarn you were just telling.

"I'm telling the truth. Every bit of that really happened," Rooster replied.

"OK, if it's true, and I'm not saying that I believe you. But if it is true, then your friend here is either dense or reckless. Sometimes it's hard to tell the difference. If you're really brave you should try the Spanish omelet. I'll come back when you're done and you can tell me if you are truly fearless or not. Come to think of it, you guys sound like you are from Minnesota, so I'd recommend the Walleye."

"Wow, you really were listening in. How did you know we were from Minneesoootta?" J.J. asked.

"Oh, I don't know. There are just some signals, ya know. But if that wasn't enough the 'uff da' was a dead giveaway. I suppose it makes a difference that I've actually been to Lake of the Woods. If you're trying to hide the fact that you're from Minneesoottta, you might want to lose the tired, old Vikings hat."

"Ouch! Sue, is it?" J.J. said, looking at her name badge. "Sue, here, is a waitress who is working hard to lose her tip," J.J. teased.

"I didn't really expect a tip because I am originally from Wisconsin, and as a dyed in the wool Packer fan it was only a matter of time until I ended up mocking the Vikings. Bye-bye tips. I knew I wasn't getting one the minute you walked in wearing that worn-out hat." She then turned and walked away.

"She didn't even ask if we really wanted the Walleye," J.J. complained.

"At this point, you'll be lucky if she brings you something edible. I'll probably have to suffer right along with you, and I'm not even a Vikings fan. OK, back to the hero story that she so rudely interrupted," Rooster demanded.

"I told you that you are just trying to make somethin' out of nothin'. Now can we just get on to something else?"

"You're not getting off that easy. Besides, we both know that we've got some time to kill before they open up the interstate. I know that there's an awesome story, and I want to hear it."

"Since you know so much, why don't you tell the story?" J.J. retorted.

Sue walked up just in time to hear the question. She looked at J.J. "I bet you're a great one at telling stories. Why don't you tell the one about Gary Anderson making every field goal and PAT in the '98 season and then missing a thirty-five-yard kick to lose their shot at the Super Bowl, or the one about Brett Favre throwing an interception with time running out in the 2010 NFC Championship Game. That one kept them out of the big show."

"Why don't you just take our order and slide that cheezehead crap back into the kitchen," J.J. said in disgust.

"Hey Sue, you can take my order any time. I'll have the Spanish omelet and my buddy here will have the Walleye. Just be sure to tell the cook that I'm no Vikings fan. I don't want any special sauces added to my food," Rooster said with a wink. "OK, you've been stretching this one out long enough. Just tell me what happened in Spud Town," Rooster challenged.

"If I tell you some of it, will you shut up about it?" J.J. fired back.

"You got it, but don't leave out the good stuff."

"Well, here's the best part. You know that I always pray the same prayer before I leave my home base. 'God please send your guardian angels before me, behind me, beside me, above and below to watch over and protect me. Keep me safe from bad drivers, drunks, texters, road hazards, animals, safe in bad weather, and alert to all dangers. Keep my rig runnin' and bring me home safe and sound.'"

"Yeah, yeah, I've heard you pray that prayer time and time again. So what?" Rooster asked, thinking J.J. was naïve to believe that angels would protect him.

"God answered that prayer in spades this time. When things started to pile up in that fog, I had just enough room on the right side of the road to slide by and come to a stop. By the time I stopped, there were a dozen vehicles piled up on the interstate beside me. I was expecting to get slammed from the back door at any second, but it just never happened. I thought the danger had passed, and I was thanking God for his protection when I saw a lady in the car next to me. The airbag had deployed and receded. She was out cold. I thought she was in trouble and I'd better get her out of that car and see if I could help. I jumped outta the rig and was able to pry her door open. I was wrong about the pileup being over. One crash after another just kept stacking up. She was pretty light, so I lifted her outta the car and up into my cab. I figured that the trailer would give us some protection if someone came flying in from the backside. That's it, end of story. When she came to, she knew she had been in an accident but didn't know how she got in my cab. That took a little explaining, but in the end she was grateful. It took all morning to clear the wreck, and she was taken to the hospital for observation. My rig didn't get touched, and when things were cleared I rolled on. I can't believe that you even heard about this. It was no big deal," J.J. humbly stated.

"No big deal? No big deal? You probably saved that woman's life. At the very least you kept her from really getting hurt. This story has been all over the chatter box. You coulda been killed. I bet this story finds the newspaper in Spud Town. That whole thing is amazing. You and your rig come out of a forty-six-car pileup without a scratch. You can thank your lucky stars on that one," Rooster exclaimed.

"You know better, Rooster. Lucky stars have nothing to do with it. God answered my prayers."

"You don't really believe that God has time to dispatch angelic protection for you and your rig, do you?"

"I absolutely do. What do you think, that God's angelic host is up in heaven with nothin' to do but strum on their golden harps? Read your Bible, Rooster. God says that He will give his angels charge over you to guard you in all your ways. You'll find it in the Psalms and that their job is to render service to God's children. You'll find that in Hebrews. I'm just asking for their help and God says, 'Ask and you will receive.' He's never failed me yet and I've been rollin' down the road for over two decades," J.J. boldly said.

"Are you saying that you haven't been in an accident in over twenty years?"

"A few dings rollin' through some tight spots in the big cities and one sidewinder when a gal shot through an intersection, but I've never been hurt. God has always had my back. I can't tell you how many times I've been plucked from the arms of death."

"See, that's what I'm talkin' about, true blue hero stuff. You can't keep yourself away from it."

"I was there and she needed help. Anyone would do that. Did you expect me to hang out in the safety of the cab?" J.J. asked.

"Nope, I would expect that you would run out into the middle of a massive pileup with no regard for life or limb and walk away like nothin' happened."

"You're looking in the wrong direction. You need a lane change man. You're looking across at me like I was doing somethin' when you should be lookin' up to see what God was gettin' done.

"Well if you've got such an inside track with God, maybe you could get the interstate opened up for us," Rooster said, with a little sarcasm.

Just then Sue came to the table with their order. "You're right," she said, "God has his part and without Him you might as well stay at home. But it sounds like when the call to duty arrives, you step up and do

117

your part. It's kinda like my role here. I can take your order, try to get it right, give it to the cook, and bring it out to you. But without the cook, you guys would still be hungry. God makes the food grow, but someone has to harvest it, truck it over here, cook it up, and deliver it. God is kinda like my Packers. They always deliver when it counts."

"Oh, you mean like the playoff game they lost to the Eagles in 1960, or the Super Bowl that they lost to the Broncos in '97, or the wild card game they lost with eight seconds to go against the Niners in '98, or the fifty-two points they gave up to Arizona in 2010, or ..."

"OK, you can stop right there. You really don't want to get me started on heartbreak and the Minnesota Vikings, do you?"

"Yeah well, unlike our football teams, my God has promised to never fail me nor forsake me. He's never missed a play in answer to my call," J.J. confidently stated.

"OK, preacher man, time to get off the pulpit and back into real life," Rooster challenged.

"You guys good here?" Sue asked. When they nodded, she turned to help at another table.

"Sure, let's talk about you for a change. How's your new job working out? Are you making any real money as an independent?" J.J. asked.

"It's great when I get the right load. Some days I have to sit around waiting for a load, and it's not only boring, but cuts into my bottom line," Rooster complained.

"Nice to be footloose and fancy free," J.J. said, with a smile. "Why did you leave Toppers Express anyway? It seemed like you were really rolling in the green stamps."

118

"Yeah, they wanted me to keep two comic books, and I just wouldn't do that. They told me that everybody is doing it, and I was stupid not to make up time. I wasn't going to risk my rig so that they could turn a profit."

"So they were cookin' the books. Did you ever challenge them on that?"

"I tried once, but they said that I could never prove it. And if I ever tried, I would be walkin' out the door. It ticked me off, but I knew that if I challenged them in any way they would bust my reputation, and I'd have to run on my own. They have enough traction that I wouldn't be able to get a company truck."

"Did you ever think about reporting them to the DOT?" J.J. questioned.

"Nah, they were right. In the end it would come down to my word against theirs. They had the power and the influence, so I just walked away."

"So they just get their way 'cause they're in control. I've heard that story before. It seems to me that the whole world is rollin' down that road. That must've hurt."

"Yeah. And the worst of it was that the guys at the top claimed to be Christians. That's what hurt the most. It took me a while to choke that one down, but in the end there was nothing I could do. So I left it with God. When they asked for my job ticket I could have made a fuss. But what good would that really do? I would end up sullying their reputation, mine and God's in one fell swoop," Rooster said, with sadness in his voice.

Just then Sue walked up. "The guys are getting the report that I-

119

94 has opened up. Just thought you guys would want to know. Are you looking to get rollin' before the next storm hits, or would you like me to set you up with another cup of java?"

"It's a sweet offer, seein' as I like having a Packer fan clean up after me," J.J. said with a smile, "but I'm already late gettin' home."

"Yeah, we're used to cleaning up on Vikings fans. You guys keep the shiny side up and the dirty side down. I'll catch you next time you are passing through," she said.

"Count on it, Sue. I run 94 a lot," Rooster said

As they went up to the counter to pay, J.J. said, "Don't forget to put your guardian angels on duty before you head down the road."

"You really think it's going to make a difference?" Rooster inquired.

"Works for me, man. I'll tell you what. You try it every time you get ready to take off. Do it for one year and then we'll compare notes. How does that sound? Put a little faith into it, all right?" J.J. asked.

"You're on. Catch you on the flip side." Rooster said, as he walked out the door.

~ ~

As he rolled out of town, Rooster remembered the last thing J.J. had said about putting the guardian angels on duty. He wasn't sure if that kind of thing actually worked, but he had made a deal with J.J. *How did that go again? God please send your guardian angels before me, behind me, beside me, above and below to watch over and protect me. Keep me safe from bad drivers, drunks, texters, road hazards, animals, safe in bad weather, and alert to all dangers. Keep my rig runnin' and bring me home safe and sound,* he prayed. *That should just about cover it,* Rooster thought. *Now if I could just catch up to J.J., I could roll in behind him and slipstream to save some fuel.*

Rooster put the pedal to the metal in spite of the snowpack and snow pillows crossing the road. He filled his mind with memories of all the crazy things that he and J.J. had done when they were young.

Someone interrupted his dream world by calling him out on the C.B. "Breaker 1-9, to the Anteater headed east on 94. There's a bear at your back door. Better back it down. Flying Ace over."

Rooster realized the heads up was for him, so he dropped back down to the speed limit and thanked the caller. It was apparent he wasn't going to catch J.J., so he decided to stop at the Tiger Truck Stop in Dickenson for a bite to eat. He realized that despite the long stop in Wibaux, he had not taken time to fuel up. As he started to fuel, he walked around his rig and found a puddle of coolant on the ground. *Oh great!* he thought. *Just what I need, a breakdown in the middle of nowhere. I don't have time for this. I'm supposed to deliver this load to Winnipeg by tomorrow, and I have customs to get through. So much for God helping me keep my rig runnin'.*

Rooster went inside to pay for the fuel and to find where he could get someone to work on his truck. The casher told him there was a Peterbuilt shop on the other side of the interstate. Rooster decided to check it out and then come back for something to eat. The Peterbuilt shop had everything Rooster might need. He was amazed to see a shop like this just outside the badlands. There wasn't a major metropolitan center anywhere near this place. *How in the world do they keep this place*

121

up and runnin'?

They offered to take a look at his rig, and the guy at the counter offered him a ride back to the Tiger Truck Stop.

Rooster thought he could a get light snack while the truck was being looked at, and if he was lucky he could stay somewhat close to schedule. While he ate, he stewed about how the timing of this problem couldn't be worse. *So much for J.J.'s magic prayer.* The more he thought about it, the more his anger churned at J.J. and at God.

After he finished eating, he picked up a ride back to the Peterbuilt shop. As he walked through the doors, he was frustrated at the thought of the possible delay and additional expense. The man at the counter was smiling, which made Rooster even more upset. He thought, *Sure, he's happy. He's about to get a big payday.*

The service man looked at Rooster and said, "Cheer up, I've got good news for you. You've got to be the luckiest guy on the road."

"Yeah, why's that?" Rooster said with disgust.

"Well, the mechanic who specializes on your kind of rig was headed out the door just as you drove in. He decided to stay and take a look. He never does that. When he's done with his shift he's always out the door and on the way to the bar. But for some reason he decided to stay. When he found out what was going on, he found that the very part needed for your repair came into the shop yesterday. If you would have had this problem a few days ago, we would have needed to wait until it came from the depot. That could have cost you a couple of days."

His anger changed to embarrassment. He teared up as he thought about what just happened. In his heart he had mocked the idea that God might help him keep his rig runnin', but he knew at this very moment that it was true. Some might think it was a coincidence or just plain luck, but Rooster knew better. He couldn't wait to tell J.J. about this the next time they connected. He gave a short prayer of thanksgiving to God and invited the angels to protect him as he pulled back onto the interstate and started rollin' toward The Peg.

A Closer Walk

As the sky darkened and jagged shards of lightening preceded the roar of thunder from the not too distant hills, he and his sister searched for sanctuary from the impending storm. The arroyo that descended from the hills had been their easiest path back home. The large, warm raindrops from the summer clouds had at first been pleasing and welcome. But as they continued to fall, they spawned the beginnings of what Blake recognized as a potential flash flood. They climbed as high as the rocky outcroppings would allow and had taken shelter in a cave.

As the water rose, the light from the cave's opening began to fade. Blake instinctively took his sister's hand and spoke softly to her. Diminished capacity was one of the terms Blake had heard used to describe Sandy. Those with less tact would say retarded. She was only eight years old, as sweet and loving as anyone you would want to meet, and lived in a world akin to a preschooler. She loved to roam the hills with Blake. They discovered and rediscovered the miracles of nature, sharing moments more precious than gold. Their dusty, little town was less than fifty miles from Tucson, but seemed more like a thousand when one considered that many of the homes had neither running water nor electricity.

The turbid water roiled as if boiling in a cooking pot filled with the offal of rotting animals. It climbed toward their feet threatening to engulf them. They inched higher up the ledge in the cave, backs pressed against its rocky surface, until the ceiling forced them to stop.

Blake could see that Sandy was frightened, so he began to sing his sister's favorite hymn. "Jesus loves me, this I know ... Yes, Jesus loves me."

She immediately began to join in. It was a comfort to know that yes, He did love them, and yes, He was ever present with them. Sometimes Blake wondered who could judge when someone had diminished capacity. Often it seemed that concerning things of real value, like love, Sandy had a far greater capacity than those who judged her. Although seemingly frail, Sandy was also resilient and of strong character. She was able to simplify complex situations and address them in a childlike but effective way. In Blake's opinion, people often overcomplicate and overanalyze, making things seem more difficult than they really are.

Debris of all kinds floated to the surface as the water finally subsided. Rotting carcasses of small animals, wood, bones and feathers of unfortunate birds made the putrid stew seem something like a dinner from hell. Blake could almost imagine that in ancient times a witch had used the cave as a place to practice her black arts. Sandy was crying softly, clutching her stuffed toy to her bosom as she too surveyed the liquid that held them prisoner.

A short time later, a small crescent of light began to illuminate the cave. It grew larger and brighter as the water dropped.

"Sun," Sandy said, in a matter-of-fact voice. Light would have been a more accurate description, since the clouds still hid the sun.

"Yes, sun," Blake agreed.

"Good," she said, "I'm cold. More sun."

They moved down a few steps where the ledge became wider. Blake took off his windbreaker and wrapped it around his sister.

"Warm," she said, feeling his body heat on her bony shoulders.

As the water receded, a full quarter of the cave's mouth was open. Blake figured that the canyon below was still a torrent of rushing, muddy water. He hoped that the storm had passed and that the sky would begin to clear. If the storm did move out of the valley it would mean that no one would miss them for several hours. He guessed their mother would not begin to seriously worry until late into the night. Even then, it would take time to convince the county sheriff to get a search party together. He put down the toe of his boot until it touched water. He noticed it had already lowered several inches. Blake thanked God and shared the information with his sister who was of course immediately ready to leave.

"We go home?" Sandy asked.

"Soon, but we have to wait until the water goes away."

"Where does the water go?"

Blake gave it some thought before answering. "I don't know. Next time we go for a walk we will do a search and try to find out where it goes."

Her smile lit up the cave. "We'll go look for it," she said.

Nearly an hour passed as they sang every hymn they could remember. Just as the sun was dipping below the horizon, Blake crawled down off the ledge onto the rocky floor of the cave. He lifted Sandy down, handed her his last stick of Juicy Fruit gum, and gave her a hug. The trail leaving the cave paralleled the outcropping for a short distance while the valley below fell sharply away. This allowed them to maintain their elevation and stay above the still raging water as they descended from the ridge.

The moon was full, and a million stars twinkled in the sky by the time they came over the rise and saw the lights of the small town.

"Hungry," Sandy announced. "Sandy's hungry."

"Blake's hungry too. I'd like some soup and hot chocolate."

He could see her smile in the moonlight as they walked hand in hand toward the town.

~ ~

"I have been really worried," their mother said, as they entered the house.

"I am sorry, Mother," Blake answered. "We got caught in the rain and had to take refuge in a cave."

"It was dark," Sandy said, as she sat at the kitchen table, warming her hands around a cup of hot chocolate.

Both Blake and his mother smiled at her comment, but said nothing. On one burner of the electric range a saucepan held two cans of Campbell's Best, still being warmed.

"Quite a storm," Blake finally said. "It blew in quickly from the mountains. Is there any damage in town?"

"They warned us to stay in our homes and off the streets," his mother said. "The road looked like a canal for a short time but finally drained away. There's a lot of debris that washed down from the hills and into the streets."

"We were probably lucky that we were still higher up on the hill," Blake said, mostly to himself as his mother sat the steaming bowls of soup on the table. Sandy already had her head bowed and was waiting for their mother to bless the food.

It was only a few minutes after eleven, but seemed later because the events of the day had used up a great deal of their energy. After eating, Sandy went to the sofa and fell fast asleep while Blake helped his mother clean up from dinner.

"Will she go to school this year?" Blake asked his mother.

"Special needs," his mother answered as though talking to herself. "I've spoken to the school board about it. They suggested Tucson where they already have a special needs program. But I can't imagine how I could work and get her to and from school."

"I'll be sixteen in a month," Blake announced with pride. "Maybe I can get a provisional license and help out by driving her."

His mother shook her head. It was evident she had already given the matter a great deal of thought. "First, there's the matter of the extra cost of insurance, and then the matter of your own schooling," she said.

"I'm not sure what we can do."

~ ~

Myron Hemstreet lived a few doors down the road from Beth and her children. He was widower who kept to himself. He could often be seen working in his yard when the weather allowed. The rest of the year the house looked deserted.

Myron sat by himself in the small community church and usually left right after the service, unwilling to linger and get involved socially. It was common knowledge that he had taken early retirement from his teaching career when his wife had fallen ill. He remained her companion and caregiver until her death. He never returned to his position with the school system.

"Hi, I'm Sandy," she said, as she took a chair beside him. "I am your neighbor."

Hemstreet eyed her cautiously as he noticed Beth and Blake take the two open seats beside her. He inclined his head in greeting toward Beth as their eyes met, but he said nothing.

"What is your name?" Sandy asked, when he did not reply.

He couldn't help but be drawn by the blue eyes and infectious smile on the little girl's face. "Myron, Mr. Hemstreet."

"I'm eight," Sandy declared, unwilling to let the conversation drop. "How old are you?"

He wanted to ignore her questions, hoping that her mother would put an end to them, but reluctantly replied, "I'm very old."

"You wouldn't look so old if you'd smile," she said, trying to sound grown up. "Mom says that smiles keep us young."

Myron smiled in spite of himself. "Your mother is a smart woman."

"Do you still live all alone?" Sandy asked. "Mom says you live all by yourself."

Myron wished more than ever that her innocent questions were directed elsewhere and looked at Beth to see if she might bring them to a close. She was busy singing along with the worship team, absorbed in worship, and unaware of their continuing dialogue.

"Yes, my wife died and my children live far away."

"I'm sorry. Would you like to come over for dinner? We can keep you company."

"Let's sing," Myron replied, trying to change the subject. "This is one of my favorites."

She smiled and began to sing "Jesus Loves Me" in the most beautiful voice he had ever heard, while the remainder of the congregation sang "The Old Rugged Cross."

Myron couldn't help but laugh out loud as several around them turned their disapproving gaze toward them. With a smile remaining on his face, he joined her. "Jesus loves me this I know 'cause the Bible tells me so ..."

Sandy smiled at him and said, "See. You look a lot younger already."

The song finished and they sat down. As the pastor led them in prayer, Sandy reached over and joined hands with Myron. Her head was bowed and her lips were moving.

Where did this kid come from? Myron thought. *Why hadn't her parents taught her any manners?* Beside her, he noted, her mother and brother were praying quietly. The sermon was focused on gifts of the Spirit, principally those mentioned in First Corinthians chapters 12 and 14.

As always Myron took notes, double-checked passages against what the pastor preached, and marked passages for his future consideration. *The pest sitting beside me must have run out of questions,* he thought. He was thankful she was silent during the message.

As the message concluded and people began to stand and leave, Sandy said in a loud voice, "Mom, I invited Mr. Myron to dinner. Is that OK?"

Beth turned to Myron, looking slightly surprised and embarrassed. "Of course. What time can we expect you, Mr. Hemstreet?"

"What time will be convenient?" he replied.

"Is six all right?

"Six will be fine," he said in a genteel manner. "May I bring dessert?"

"That would be fine. I'm sure the kids would really enjoy that."

~ ~

It was nearing the Christmas break at school. The snow was ankle deep, and the desert nights were cold and clear. Beth had decorated the house, but had not yet purchased a tree, hoping prices would be reduced as Christmas neared. Presents were wrapped and hidden away from curious eyes.

131

A knock came at the door. Blake turned on the porch light and opened the door. Mr. Hemstreet stood on the stoop holding a nice fir tree in one hand and a box in the other.

"I took a chance that you had not already purchased a tree," he said, entering with a smile and looking around the room.

Beth and Sandy came out of the kitchen and joined Blake and their guest.

"Oh, Mr. Myron, that is a beautiful tree," Sandy said. Her eyes sparkled. "Is it for me?"

"It is for all of you," Myron said, smiling, "and these too," he added, setting the box down. Inside were several neatly wrapped packages. "Sandy, can you read the nametags?"

It had been nearly three months since they first began to spend each school day together. He was taking joy in teaching, and she enjoyed learning. After that first Sunday dinner had brought them together, they had all become close friends and valued companions.

For the first time in years, Myron celebrated the season with heartfelt joy, relishing the gifts he was able to both give and receive.

Drama I

When I asked what I could do for him, the graying man in the sweatshirt replied, "Just a place to lay my head."

I run a small boarding house in an area that has become out of the way ever since the four-lane changed the traffic flow and dried up the tourist trade for our little town. With the emphasis on mpg and everyone's desire to get where they are going yesterday, few travel the extra 500 feet to stop in our little burg. Oh, they might stop and buy a conscience purchase now and then, if their children need to use a restroom or a few gallons from the local station to get them to the city where prices are cheaper. But they never buy anything significant.

I inherited the business free and clear, which was the only thing that made it possible keep the doors open. It does, however, provide suitable housing for me. It also requires plenty of routine maintenance, keeping me active after my retirement from the Navy. The high plains of northern Idaho where grain and row crops flourish had gradually gone from family farms to large corporations. The out-of-state owners fly in several times a year to shoot the bountiful Chinese pheasants. They bring clients and guests with them, none of whom would stay in my shabby accommodations. There are a few traveling up from southern Idaho in search of whitetails who might spend a night or two.

"Glad to have ya," I said with enthusiasm. "How long you planning to stay?"

"Can't say," he answered. "That's up to the Lord."

Appreciating the company, but not desiring a debate I ignored his answer.

"I furnish two meals and the room for forty-five dollars a night, if you're not too picky about the food."

"Sounds more 'n fair," he said, laying two twenties and a five on the worn counter. "I 'spect I missed breakfast already."

"It's just you and me this morning. No trouble to fix you a plate of bacon and eggs if that suits you."

In truth I was glad for his company. I'd have been happy to cook even if he wasn't a guest.

"Ben, Ben Smith," he said, smiling and sticking his weathered hand over the counter.

"Charlie Burns," I said. "Glad to meet you."

That is how we met one Wednesday morning in May of 2010, a day I'm not likely to forget.

Ben joined me in the kitchen where we made small talk while I fried up the kind of food our mothers warned us about.

"Wheat or white?" I asked. "And how do you like your eggs?"

"Don't much matter," he said. "The chemo takes the flavor out of the food."

I hadn't noticed until he took off his ball cap that it covered a nearly bald head.

"Cancer?" I asked, noticing the yellowish tinge to his skin.

"Prostate, but it has spread around some."

He didn't seem unwilling to talk about it, and not at all self-pitying.

"Seems like it's a trade off. Either you're a woman and fight breast cancer, or a man and this thing."

He nodded but added nothing to my observation.

"You're a pretty good hand with the spatula," he said, observing me as I turned his eggs and scattered the hash browns across the flattop.

"Had a little practice in the Navy," I answered. "Twenty-three years aboard ship and finally made chief."

He smiled at that. "I's a gunner," he said proudly. "Made Second Class my first cruise. Saw a lot of the Delta on a PBR."

With breakfast plated, I poured two cups of coffee and joined him at the table. As we talked I learned that he was just mustering out when I boarded my first ship and headed out in 1967. I guessed that he was in his 70s, not by looks, but more by the timing of the events we shared. We continued to talk while I cleared the table and washed up the dishes. I was looking directly at him when pain filled his face, causing him to stop mid-sentence. He reached under his sweatshirt and pressed a button, releasing a measure of painkiller into his bloodstream. Within seconds his smile returned and he apologized for the interruption.

"I hate to do it," he said, "but sometimes it's just easier to let the medicine do its work."

Over the next few days I'd see Ben about town, coming and going, visiting with folks, and making friends.

On Friday when we had just sat down to breakfast, he smiled and asked, "How many rooms do you have ready for visitors?"

"I have twenty total, but only make up the rooms as they are needed. As you may have noticed, we don't have a lot of company."

He nodded his understanding. "Do you have anyone to help you when you have several guests?"

I was wondering why he posed the question, but I didn't ask. "Rosa has always been eager to earn a few extra bucks when I have asked. Her husband left her here alone with two children and never looked back. She works part time at the mercantile and babysits when the need arises."

"Charlie," Ben said, smiling, "please call her and get all the rooms ready as soon as you can."

I must have looked doubtful because he said, "Please trust me on this. I'll pay her wages."

Surprised and curious, I asked, "What have you got up your sleeve, Ben? I have noticed you cruising around town speaking to folks."

Ben smiled mischievously. "I like your little town and the people, but it appears that you are all just sitting around treading water, waiting for someone to throw the dirt over you."

He was looking me right in the eye as he spoke, and I knew he was talking directly to me. My first reaction was defensive, to respond with excuses. But the longer I hesitated, the more I knew it was true.

"Summerville is a beautiful, little town. I wish I had come here before I got sick. I'd like to try and breathe life back into it if I can."

I was intrigued. "What do you have in mind?"

"I haven't got it all worked out yet, but God has given me some ideas. Did you see my new Lincoln out front?"

"Yeah," I answered, looking out the window again at the beautiful, new SUV.

Ben began telling me his life story. "My wife and I couldn't have children," he said, looking down at the floor. "We did well financially and had a great life together until she passed two years ago. When I found out about my cancer, I just liquidated everything, sold the house and furniture, and kept the few things that held any value to me. Everything I own is in the car outside or in a bank account." He stopped for a moment then continued. "I have found that money can seldom fix things, but with God's blessing it can be used to help people fix themselves."

I looked at him, considered what he had just said, then nodded.

"I've got an idea," he said. "I've been talking to some folks about it. Nearly everyone I've spoken to is on board. In the past I have been deeply involved in shooting sporting clays. I was president of the Western Association at one time. I have spoken to Pastor Glenn and we are working on having the church sponsor a skeet shoot with the benefits going to charity. I know I can count on at least fifty participants by making a few calls, maybe more. They'll bring their motor homes, family and friends, eager to have a relaxing and enjoyable time in your little town. I have seven premier shotguns in the car. I plan to use six of them as prizes for six division winners who'll pay a fee of one hundred dollars to compete. Then, I have a clear title to the Lincoln that will interest the "big boys," the real professionals, who will pay a thousand dollars for a chance to win it and the bragging rights."

I must have been smiling because he smiled back and continued.

"Do you remember how Jesus used the fish and loaves to feed

the multitude?" he asked.

I nodded, unclear of the connection.

"If I liquidated everything today and gave the town a check, it might be a couple of hundred thousand. A short time later we'd all be broke and the town would still have the same problems."

"Give a guy a fish, or teach him to fish," I said, remembering the analogy.

"Charlie," he asked, "why do you suppose some folks have so much trouble believing in Jesus and coming to the faith?"

Once again, I wasn't following his logic.

"With men we have learned that if it seems too good to be true, it usually is," he said. "We distrust people who proclaim that His love would make Him willing to come and die for us. We can't accept the idea that just by asking for forgiveness and turning to God we can have eternal life. We think there must be something hidden in the small print somewhere that says we must work to deserve that love."

"If it's free or too cheap, something must be wrong with it," I said.

"Raise your room rates fifteen or twenty dollars a night," he said, giving me a wink. "When they rent a room, they get a discount coupon to use across the street at the station if they fill up. Mike has agreed that for every full tank of gas he sells he'll give a coupon for savings on a room. Beth and Don at the grocery store are partnering with the motel at the other end of town in the same way. The diner is pledging ten percent of their gross to the church and giving away a chance to win one of my rifles with every fifty dollars in meal purchases. They'll have a drawing after the final event of the competition."

He named off other local businesses, said how they had agreed to contribute, and explained how they stood to benefit. "Time's short. We need to get word out and get things organized."

When he finished, I called Rosa. She agreed to help out.

"You'll need food," Ben said. "Good stuff and lots of it. But, buy as much as you can in town before ordering outside."

I nodded, seeing his point to buy local even if the cost was higher.

"Where do you buy your gas?" Ben asked.

"I usually fill up in Sandpoint when I make a run to get supplies. Then I use Mike in between times," I admitted, feeling guilty for my answer.

He didn't need to say any more to make his point. If Mike sold more volume he could sell cheaper. If he sold cheaper, he would increase his volume. I saw myself suddenly as both the problem and the answer to the town's woes.

Ben smiled, apparently appreciating my honesty. "You've gotta get a new mindset, the lot of you. You'll sink or swim together."

~ ~

Behind the scenes Ben was busy making calls, buying newspaper advertising, having the local print shop make flyers, and getting word out on Facebook and Twitter. The event was still two weeks away when he gathered the town at the community church for a potluck. It was the food that brought us together, but it was the promise of a future that brought kinship and smiles to the tired faces. It seemed that everyone had a stake, from the Girl Scouts who hung notices on the cars at the shopping area in Sandpoint, to the Elks Club who challenged their brothers at lodges across the state. Everyone seemed to have an angle, an idea, a friend or relative somewhere that needed what we had to offer. Ben invited representatives from gun manufacturers and ammunition dealers to come and hawk their wares for an expected charitable donation.

Rosa had my place shipshape with freshly made beds, towels, and nary a cobweb to be seen. She agreed to help serve and clean up, and her two teenage sons would bus tables. Our walk-in cooler and both freezers were filled with prime cuts and fresh fruits and vegetables from our local supplier. The final few days seemed to fly by. The locals began to frequent each other's establishment, bringing with them a few bucks and a sense of commitment to the cause.

Four days before the Memorial Day weekend they began to arrive. First the retirees in big motor homes and fifth-wheel trailers, followed by those needing accommodations arriving in festive moods and with open checkbooks. While my boarding house atmosphere must have seemed quaint to those from the big cities with their five-star hotels, indoor pools and saunas, it actually enhanced their whole experience.

Ben had financed, supervised, and helped build the throwing stations, which were located on a vacant lot adjacent to the church, and leased the necessary land  around it to assure safety and parking. I heard later that he gifted the land and the improvements to the church as an encouragement to continue the

140

event. The sign on the highway announced Summerville and stated its population at 195, but we knew that several families had moved since the last census and only one birth had been recorded. With ninety-four signed up to shoot the first day, and considering that few had arrived alone, I guessed that our population had doubled in less than four days.

Although Ben may not have known everyone, everyone knew him…or of him. Apparently he held many records in the ranks of trap shooters and some with rifled barrels as well. All of my rooms were filled, just as he had predicted. I elected to stay out back in my travel trailer when the last guest checked in. I called the motel at the far end of town and found they were turning guests away and placing them in private homes and available mobile units.

Ben had the first round of eliminations scheduled to begin Friday afternoon, followed by a meet and greet time in the park. The second and third rounds would begin early on Saturday and continue until dark. Everyone would take Sunday off, hopefully to hear Pastor Glenn and spend some of their surplus cash locally. Monday was reserved for the finals, presentations, and an awards ceremony where the fortunate could sport their trophies and brag to their brethren of their prowess with the smooth bores.

By Thursday night I was already running low on meat, so I called the local butcher, who in turn called his brother who was a rancher. He arranged an additional rear quarter for me. When I closed out the till, to my surprise I had grossed nearly $1,500 a day for the previous three days. Of course I had not yet paid Rosa, her sons, or the food suppliers. I set the money in my lockbox until I could make a run to the bank. I held back four hundred dollars with the intention of leaving it at the church for tithe Sunday morning. I was eager to share the good news with Ben.

Friday morning I served six dozen eggs, twenty-five pounds of fresh hash browned spuds, and thirty-six petite steaks along with a few pounds of bacon, a mountain of toast and boatload of coffee.

Immediately after cleanup, I put three nice prime rib roasts in the oven on low heat, wrapped fifty-five russet bakers in foil, and prepared four dozen servings of fresh picked asparagus to be cooked for the evening meal.

The pop, pop of shot shells echoed in the distance as I walked along the street lined with vehicles sporting out-of-state plates. I crossed over to Mike's where he was busily washing windows and checking fluids the way all service stations had done twenty years ago. He had two vehicles being filled and a fifth wheeler waiting in line when I arrived.

"How's it going, Mike?" I asked.

He gave me a big smile. "Busier than a one-armed paperhanger. I've already sold more today than all of last month."

I noticed that he had hired a couple of local boys and had shown them the basics of the business. One was checking tires, and the other had washed the windows and was checking the oil while the pump continued filling the tank on a massive motor home. He gave me another smile as I started back across to my boarding house.

"Are you going to have any left after you feed your guests?" Mike asked. "I've been smellin' it cookin' all day."

"I'll make sure I do. You and Claire can come on over after you close and enjoy prime rib. It'll be my treat."

"It's a date," he said, smiling broadly. "I'll call her when I get a break and let her know."

As I walked into the kitchen I could tell what he'd been talking about as the aroma of the roasting beef filled my nostrils. I broke down four whole chickens, knowing that some of the guests preferred it that way. I peeled a dozen potatoes and hand cut them into home fries. I was enjoying cooking again. It was a challenge to plan and prepare meals for large groups of people. I felt confident that after burgers and dogs in the park and a full day of activity, a good sit down meal would be appreciated. As I dumped the washed and peeled roots from the horseradish in the food processor, I reminded myself to breathe through my mouth rather than my nose.

Rosa came up behind me and inhaled a sinus full of the pungent root, causing tears to run down both cheeks. I shooed her away and suggested that she might do better if she set the tables and prepared the beverages out of the kitchen until the dust settled a bit. I added a dollop of mayo, a dash of salt, and a tablespoon of pickle juice to the blender and found myself with a quart of quite respectable horseradish sauce. I began the au jus sauce with a prepared mix, intending to fortify and complete it with the natural juices from the roasts when they came out of the oven. Seven loaves of artisan bread sat on the countertop waiting to be sliced and looking like little, brown, half basketballs.

With things under control, I joined Rosa in the dining area where she had stopped tearing, but was still flushed from the horseradish.

"Are you and the boys keeping track of your hours?" I asked. "I'd like them to help serve again tonight if they don't already have plans."

"We've been writing them down on the calendar at home," she

said. "I already asked them to keep their schedules open in case you asked."

"Thank you," I said, returning her smile as I began to set out water glasses and coffee cups on the tables.

I hadn't noticed until then that Rosa was quite attractive. She had dark hair and eyes that spoke of Latin heritage. There was an energy about her that belied her age, an enthusiasm for life that had helped her overcome life's difficulties.

"What do you think of all of this?" I asked, referring to the town's big event.

"Smells good," she answered, playing dumb.

"I mean how the town is full of people and how all of us have joined together to make it all work."

She smiled. "I knew what you meant. I hope it's not a one-time thing."

I nodded. "Me too. I haven't seen so many smiles among the townsfolk since we won the state basketball championship."

"Did we win state?" she asked unwittingly. "I don't remember that."

This time it was me who was teasing her. "I don't either. I meant the townsfolk have never seemed so happy."

For the first time in many years, I was flirting with a woman and enjoying it. She seemed to be enjoying our banter as well. I guessed her to be my junior by at least ten years, a fact that would have mattered a few years ago. It seemed less important now.

"We appreciate the work," she offered, looking at me with a twinkle in her eyes.

"No more than I appreciate the help. I'd like nothing more than to have you full time."

She said nothing in response, but the look she was giving me made me blush. "I mean, I hope we stay busy enough to afford full-time help."

Again she smiled mischievously. "I knew what you meant."

I excused myself by explaining that I was heading down to watch the activities and get an idea of when we might expect our dinner guests. Ben greeted me warmly, talking between the explosions of the nearby shotguns.

"We should wrap up the first round soon. Everyone enjoyed lunch, and most are just waiting to see who moves on to the next rounds. I'd say you could plan to serve at six. You should have a hungry crowd just waiting to be fed."

I returned to the kitchen, turned the ovens off, and let the roasts continue to cook as it approached rare on the thermometer. Rosa had breaded the cut-up chicken and had it ready to drop into the fryer. At five thirty laughter and conversation in the dining room announced the return of our guests. She begin slicing the bread as I went out to give them the dinner schedule. Her two boys arrived just in time to seat and begin pouring beverages for the guests, while the steamer began its magic on the tender asparagus shoots.

Four baskets of chicken went into the oil while I began to cut and plate the prime rib. Rosa finished the au jus sauce and put it on the plates in serving cups beside the horseradish, and then added the vegetable. I eyeballed the meat for color and separated the rare, medium rare and mediums, directing the boys as they served the tables. I dumped the chicken and replaced it with fries as the cooking oil regained its temperature. I was amazed at how Rosa and her sons anticipated my needs and moved with the grace of seasoned kitchen help. The chicken and fries were served family style with many of the adults helping their children. I held back seven nice cuts of prime and one full chicken for Mike, Claire and the kitchen staff to enjoy. When they showed up, it was about a quarter to seven. When Ben joined us, most of our guests had finished eating and left the dining room. We blessed the food and enjoyed our meal together.

"Tomorrow will be the busy day," Ben said, thinking aloud. "Nearly all of those in the second round will be up early and stay late. I might suggest something quick and simple for breakfast."

I nodded.

"The diner is furnishing box lunches with the women's auxiliary from the church assembling and selling them at the park. Do you have something in mind for dinner tomorrow night?" he asked.

I looked at Rosa to see if she had any ideas. She said nothing but smiled and nodded.

"We've got it covered," I said confidently, winking at her.

"Good," Ben said, sounding tired. "I'm going to hit the rack early and let some of your fine food settle a bit."

When he stood and said his good nights, I could see the day had taken its toll.

To be continued.

Drama II

"Choice of sausage patty, ham, or bacon with three pancakes and two eggs 'our way,'" the boys said, to the assembled breakfast crowd, parroting my words.

I didn't want to get into custom cooking each meal, but wanted to give them a sense of choice all the same. In less than forty minutes most had finished eating and were leaving for the shoot. Rosa helped me with the cleanup while her sons cleared the tables and swept the floor.

"Ever been married, Charlie?" Rosa asked, right out of the blue.

When I regained control, I answered, "Nope, never have."

We were working right beside each other finishing up the pots and pans and putting away those already cleaned.

"So," I said, "you seemed to have an idea for dinner. Want to share it with me?"

"What do you think about barbecue?"

"Like what? Ribs, pork, or what?"

"All of it. I make a killer sauce that can be used on all of it."

"I like it," I answered, thinking through my inventory of meats. "But we'll need to get our hands on some ribs, buns, coleslaw makin's,

147

and a few rolls of paper towels to supplement the paper napkins.

"How about baked beans?"

I looked in the pantry. "We've got two ten-pound cans of Bush's that will be nearly as good as homemade and a lot quicker. What are you going to need for your sauce?"

"Brown sugar, molasses ...," she said, mentally going through the list as she removed items from the pantry. "Do you have honey?"

"I think there's a quart in there somewhere," I answered. "When things slowed down, I went to the individual serving packets."

Rosa nodded but did not reply.

"We fed about forty last night and again this morning," I said, as much to myself as to her. "I expect we should plan for about the same tonight."

I took out a nine-pound pork butt, and cut a like-sized, boneless, round roast off the hanging quarter, preheated the oven to 250 degrees, then began seasoning them both. When they were tucked inside and beginning to cook, I called and ordered beef and pork ribs from our local butcher.

It was only ten o'clock when I picked them up and returned with a gallon of mayo, hamburger buns, and four small heads of cabbage. Rosa had her sauce simmering on low heat and offered me a taste. The ribs went into boiling salted water for twenty minutes, then drained, seasoned, and covered with sauce before joining the roasts in the oven. While Rosa ribboned the cabbage, I mixed the mayo, celery seeds, powdered sugar, and pickle juice until I was satisfied with the taste of the coleslaw dressing. Smiling, I offered Rosa a sample.

"I use vinegar, but I like the pickle juice better, and the

powdered sugar dissolves better than granulated," she said.

We seemed to be in sync and enjoying the whole kitchen experience. When noon came, she seemed in no hurry to leave. So I fixed us each a BLT and some hand-cut fries for lunch. There was no bitterness, but rather a melancholy quality to her voice as she began to talk about her early life, the failed marriage, and her sons growing up without a father figure to guide them.

"I guess we were just too young, too selfish, and not willing to make it work," she said. "It was not until I found Jesus that I stopped looking at myself as a victim and began to count my blessings at having two healthy sons."

I liked what she said, but didn't know how to respond. So I just nodded agreement.

"Twelve years he's been gone. But he's the one who lost out on the joy of knowing his sons, not me."

"You seem to have done a fine job with them," I said sincerely. "You should be proud."

"I am, but I worry now that they are becoming men whether I can provide the right kind of advice and direction for them."

It was nearly three o'clock when Ben walked in. "Smells good," he offered.

"I hope so. We've got a ton of food cooking. How are things going with the shoot?" I asked.

"Good. Everyone seems to be having a good time. We should be done and know which ones are going to the finals by five."

I nodded. "I planned dinner for around six. That should give everyone time to get back and clean up."

149

"I'm going to catch a few winks," he said. "Would you wake me at four?"

"You got it. Sleep well," I said, noticing he was moving slowly and seemed to be in pain.

~ ~

By four o'clock the ribs were done and wrapped in foil to hold in the heat. I began pulling the beef while the pork continued to bake. Rosa left to pick up her boys. Ben joined me in the kitchen, and I gave him samples.

"Good sauce," he said.

"Rosa's recipe."

"You better keep her on. That's the kind of thing that makes for a good reputation. People would drive here from the city just for a taste of that."

"Ben, I need some help here. I don't know how much to pay her and the boys."

"Thought I was paying her. I said I would."

"That's not necessary. I'm doing well and am pleased to pay her myself."

He grinned and winked. "Pay her what's fair. That's Biblical."

"And how much is that?" I asked, fearing to hear his answer.

"Your heart will tell you," he said. "You'll know."

He smiled and left, passing Rosa and her sons as they were coming in the door.

Both boys beamed as they got a nice whiff of the food.

"Barbecue!" they said as one.

Rosa smiled, and said quietly, "They love barbecue."

Rosa and her sons started setting the tables for dinner while I added the sauce to the mountain of beef and returned it to the oven. I repeated the exercise with the pork and noted the time at nearly five o'clock. Rosa joined me in the kitchen and began buttering the buns in preparation of toasting them on the grill. I stirred the bean pot.

If you've ever been in a cornfield full of geese, or frequented a barnyard with chickens, you'd recognize the sounds that began coming from the living room and dining area. Men and women in shooting jackets and excited children, all talking at once were reliving their recent experiences. I stuck my head out of the kitchen and announced dinner at six.

At exactly six o'clock, Ben tapped a spoon on the side of his water glass, calling the group to attention. He then asked the Lord's blessing on the food. Rosa and her sons brought out each type of meat, beans, and coleslaw, placing them on the tables family style. To my surprise and joy, Mike and Claire entered with sheepish looks on their faces.

"I've been smellin' it all day," Mike said. "If you have enough we'd be happy to pay."

We added two more chairs and welcomed them to a table.

"What's the plan for tomorrow?" a tall man in his 50s asked Ben.

"Tomorrow is the Lord's day. The church welcomes all who might want to hear the Word and will sponsor a potluck after the service. The finals for all categories will resume Monday morning, followed by

151

an awards ceremony."

There was discussion among the group as to how they would spend the day.

Someone asked me, "Will you serve breakfast before church?"

"I will, but it would help a lot to know how many will be at our table."

About ten planned to sleep in or had other activities in mind, and the rest pledged to be at the table at nine o'clock to eat French toast, bacon, hash browns, and eggs before church.

~ ~

The irony of Pastor Glenn's choice of sermon topics was not missed by most of the town's faithful, and by many of those who knew Ben well.

"In Matthew chapter 16, verses 24 through 27, Jesus is speaking to his disciples. 'If anyone desires to come after me, let him deny himself, and take up his cross, and follow me. For whoever desires to save his life will lose it, but whoever loses his life for my sake will find it. For what profit is it to a man, if he gains the whole world, and loses his own soul? For the Son of Man will come in the glory of His Father with His angels, and then He will reward each according to his works.'"

I stole a glance across the room at Ben, who was sitting with his head slightly bowed. A look, not of resignation or sorrow, but of joy and anticipation, was on his face. As a lump rose in my throat, I realized that Ben's homecoming was near, and that his wife and friends eagerly awaited his arrival in heaven. I choked back the tears and thought of a time long ago when a local blacksmith would have used his skills to anneal metals together before the invention of the modern welder. Ben had used his skills to anneal the hearts of our community. I had been a believer for a long time, but had not walked in His footsteps with any regularity until after I retired and moved home. As I listened and thought about Ben, I felt a new level of commitment rising within my heart.

Following the service, tables and sunshades were assembled beside the church. I noted that many of the visitors were helping the locals make ready for the feast and exchanging notes with names and phone numbers. Rosa and I restrained our urge to jump in and take over in order to get the event organized. Instead we watched as those with less experience struggled but ultimately came together in service to one other. I reflected on how life is a string of learning opportunities and a chance to grow together.

Ben was leaning against a tree surrounded by several of his cronies from the shoot.

"What do you have planned for dinner?" Rosa questioned.

"I haven't given it much thought," I answered honestly. "Any ideas?" *Of course she does or she wouldn't have asked*, I thought, but kept it to myself.

"How about some easy, greasy, finger food?" she answered. "We've only got a couple more days to clog their arteries."

I couldn't keep from laughing. "How about beer-battered finger steaks and onion rings with fries? Do you suppose that would max out their fat intake?"

"Purrrfect," Rosa answered, sounding like a lazy tomcat. "We've got a lot of leftover horseradish that we can mix with ketchup to make into a sauce."

Her sons overheard the conversation and eagerly gave their nods of approval.

It was after three when I returned to the kitchen. The potluck was over and cleanup completed. Many of the guests had gone to their rooms for a nap, while some remained in the common area visiting. Others were out seeing the sights. I had the meat marinating in the batter, the onions sliced, and some of the potatoes peeled. Rosa jumped in and began peeling while I began to cut them into fries. The boys began preparing the tables without being told.

The sheer volume of deep-fried food was overwhelming both to the cooks and to the four available fryers. We decided not to serve family style, but to plate the food as it was ready.

I put on my best chef's face and addressed those seated at the table. "Rather than have everyone wait while the food gets cold, we have chosen to feed it right out of the fryers. Some of you will eat before others, so let's bless the food in advance." As they bowed their heads, I thanked the Lord for the food.

Tubs of horseradish ketchup, a mild Thousand Island, and regular ketchup adorned the tables. Much to the enjoyment of the hungry visitors, Rosa's sons hustled to relay the food from the kitchen.

~ ~

Monday morning brought a light rain that cleared by ten o'clock. Spring sunshine quickly dried the ground. As promised the first six categories shot first, with divisions for novice, experienced, and expert for both men and women. As each champion was crowned, Ben presented the winner with a beautiful shotgun. At noon they broke for lunch, which was furnished by the diner. Everyone then returned as the eliminations began for the final category. Washed and waxed, Ben's Lincoln sat on the grass nearby with a three-foot trophy gracing its hood.

There were four finalists, each having shot perfect rounds two consecutive times the previous day. As they gathered, Ben took the bullhorn and announced the rules for the final rounds.

"Obviously I've made this too easy for you four scoundrels," he said, eliciting a laugh from the crowd. "Let's step it up a little or we'll be here until the Fourth of July. Each finalist will face away from the thrower until he says pull. No shells are to be in the gun or in the participants' hands prior to turning to face the birds."

As the finalists looked at one another, they began to smile and plan their strategies.

"We will draw straws to see in what order you will shoot. Anyone not posting a perfect round will be eliminated. Agreed?"

The four seasoned veterans agreed and gathered around Ben to draw straws.

"Blaine, you are up," Ben announced, "followed by Ernie, Ron, and Rich. If we go to a second round, we'll reverse the order and let Rich lead off."

Blaine went twenty-nine for thirty before stepping back to let Ernie replace him. Ernie dusted all thirty as did Ron. Rich had trouble loading and missed his fifth and sixth birds, stepped back and shook his head in disgust. With Rich and Blaine out, Ron led off the second round, again shooting a perfect thirty. When Ernie took his position the audience held its breath as the first twenty fell in pieces in the nearby field. He stopped to make sure he had enough shells, then broke seven more before missing his twenty-eighth bird.

The crowd roared, congratulating Ron. Ben handed Ron the keys to the Lincoln and the first place trophy. Ben called the three finalists to the podium and gave each a check for a thousand dollars, in effect, returning their entrance fees.

"I'm paying your fees for next year in advance with the hope that you all will return and enjoy another few days with this community," Ben said.

Ben closed out the awards ceremony by pulling the winning ticket in the drawing that the diner had sponsored. The winner was the father of a family of four, and the crowd applauded as he came forward to claim the prize.

~ ~

Ben stayed in the boarding house until June 10, sharing stories and his considerable wisdom with us. When he didn't join me one morning for breakfast, I went to his room and found that he had gone to his permanent residence, the one Jesus talked about when He said, "I go to prepare a place for you." As he had requested, Ben was buried in our cemetery near the church. Nearly the entire town attended the funeral.

With her sons' blessings, Rosa and I were married shortly

afterward. We changed the name of our business to "Rosa's Bar-B-Que and Bedroom" and are working together to maintain the legacy that Ben planted in our hearts.

This Memorial Day will be the fourth anniversary of Ben's dream and positive evidence that one man plus God can change the world.

Details

"The devil is in the details," he said, repeating a statement he had heard many years before. Be that as it may, details are important, and God is in the detail business. Hank remembered reading in Exodus how God laid out very specific plans for the building of His tabernacle. Minute, precise and very carefully planned, each facet of its construction was plainly laid out without room for error. Hank was a general contractor, concentrating primarily on small, commercial projects with an occasional private residence thrown in for variety. Like his father, he had been a carpenter and a jack of all trades in the early days. Out of necessity he formed and finished cement, framed and sided, hung and finished sheet rock, roofed,

 insulated, painted, and pulled most of the wire for the licensed electricians to connect. He built and finished cabinets, hung doors, and trimmed out entire houses.

Having a good working knowledge of each part of the process

gave him an advantage over many of his competitors who were less hands on and basically project managers with little training. Many were just organizers, men who hired other men to do the work, but not qualified to spot defects or know if the work had been done correctly. Defects, cut corners, and shoddy workmanship always came to light after the profits were spent and the customers had taken up residence.

Hank was a devout Christian, struggling to compete with those who cared very little about reputation or morality. More often than not, the amount of the bid determined who got the job. As a result, those whose guarantees were truly reputable were seldom awarded the contract. Often he saw it as his duty to protect his clients from themselves. He would warn them about cutting corners that would ultimately cost them more money. He remembered when one of his clients had been enraged when he tried to simultaneously use two of his power tools in his garage and had tripped the breaker. Hank's sub had used 15-amp wiring and breakers rather than the 20-amp that were specified. It cost Hank a day's labor and two hundred dollars out of pocket to fix the mistake. Lesson learned, he now inspected the wiring and plugs, making sure they were correct before they were covered with sheetrock. Whenever he lost a job on price and was tempted to cheapen the quality of his work, God brought this little lesson to mind.

As Hank aged, he looked critically at the accumulation that represented the fruits of his labors, wondering what had become of the fortunes that had come and gone over the years. It appeared that comfortable retirement was out of the question and that he would likely be forced to continue to work just to survive. His wife seldom complained, but he knew she looked longingly at their friends whose retirement seemed secure and were able to travel and enjoy time together. He felt guilty for some of his decisions to spend rather than save, to buy rather than be content with what he owned. He knew God had blessed them and the seeming shortfall was of their own doing.

~ ~

"Hi, Hank," his friend said, as he made his way into the coffee shop.

"Morning, Gary," he answered, smiling as he watched his friend fold up his walker and grab the seat across the table.

"Just coffee?" the waitress asked as she turned over their cups and filled them automatically.

Hank looked across at his friend who was looking over the menu. "Give us a minute," he said.

She smiled and went to a neighboring table.

"How's Barb?" Gary asked, as he always did.

"Doing fine," Hank answered automatically. "She said to tell you hi."

"You're lucky to have her."

"I know," Hank said laughing. "I'm reminded of it every morning by either you or her."

"I mean it. I'd give anything to have Freda back."

After his wife, Freda, died of cancer, the two met four or five mornings a week to share time and food and provide support for each other. Freda was Hank's younger sister. Not only was Gary his brother-in-law, he was his longtime, best friend.

"How's the leg doing?" Hank asked.

"It's about the same. It is still weak and tires out easily. I do pretty well when I first get up and around, but as the day wears on it begins to drag. I feel like an old man."

"You are an old man," Hank said laughing. "We both are."

"When do you suppose that happened?" Gary asked. "One day we're playing softball and the next we can hardly get out of bed."

The two men visited, laughed and ate before heading their separate ways. Gary went home and Hank to a job site. He still called it a job site, though it was just a patio cover he was working on. It would take him two days unless they wanted him to paint it. He'd clear a couple hundred dollars on this job, which would help pay the bills.

~ ~

"You're out," the umpire said, as the runner tried to make home.

The tag had been clean and his effort to dislodge the ball from Gary's grip by sliding into him had been futile. The game ended at six to five. Hank had pitched four perfect innings before the other team had figured him out. The Cougars' unbeaten streak had nearly been ruined when they fell behind by one in the seventh. They came back in the ninth to go up by one before taking the field. The Braves had one on and two out when their man stole second. The batter hit a line drive just over second to short centerfield. The centerfielder took it on one hop and threw for home where Gary fielded the ball and tagged the runner.

The roar of the home crowd welcomed them, and the smiling faces of Freda and Barb beamed at them through the little diamonds of

161

the chain-link fence in the backstop. Senior year meant every moment counted. All of the experiences leading up to this had been designed by some higher power to magnify this time of life. Hank believed that, and repeated it to his team before every game.

"This is our moment, our defining moment. These are the times we will always look back on and know what we were meant to do," he said.

The class president had stolen much of Hank's speech and repeated it at graduation to parents who had never heard it. Gary had gone on to college and earned a degree in engineering. He worked for the power and light company for thirty-five years before retiring early because of a stroke.

Hank had always liked to work with his hands and learned the trade from his own father. He went to junior college nights and worked days. He and Barb started dating in the ninth grade and married the fall after graduation. Their first year was hard; she had miscarried in her fifth month and both were heartbroken. When Freda became pregnant and had a daughter, the families celebrated together. When Barb had sons, they likewise shared the joy.

Hank was just thirty when his father was killed in a car accident. His mother was only fifty and had never worked outside the home. She lacked the desire and skills to find a full time job. Hank's die was cast. His responsibility to care for his own family and provide for his mother was clear. With both sons in school, Barb took a part-time job as a receptionist at the power company. Hank's mother watched the boys when they came home from school and fixed dinner for the family. As his business grew and prospered, Hank built a cottage on the property to allow his mother a place of her own.

It was Hank's mother who had first suggested that they go to church. Up to that point, their only thought of spirituality had been trying to observe the Golden Rule. It seemed that the loss of her husband had opened a door to her heart and revealed an emptiness that needed to be filled. Hank, Barb and the rest of the family didn't feel the same calling, but were comfortable with the idea and often went with her. She accepted the Lord and was baptized that same year. The rest of the family found themselves too busy with life to get actively involved or truly pursue God, until the children began asking questions and showing an interest.

Gary and Hank were struggling to hold on to their youth as they neared forty, playing sports and spending leisure time at the gym pretending they were still young and fit. Both of their careers provided for them financially, giving them an excess of things that drew them away from God and toward self-indulgence. Hank bought a boat and Gary bought a cabin, which ultimately demanded that they use and enjoy them. Even the children were drawn to the excitement of water skiing, fishing, camping and the outdoors.

Hank's oldest son, Max, was the victim of an error in judgment that cost him his life. He was at a party where he tried crack cocaine one time and suffered a heart attack. He died at age fifteen. His younger brother felt orphaned, as both parents withdrew from him in their grief. Only his grandmother was there to provide the support he so badly needed.

Hank began to drink and spend long hours at work, while Barb tried to find companionship with her co-workers. Were it not for his mother's influence, they'd have lost their marriage. She began reading the Bible each night to her grandson. Gradually Barb joined them, listening in and asking questions. Hank would come home, often smelling of alcohol, and see his family sitting together sharing the moment. He made excuses and chose to stay home alone rather than attend church with his family.

However, a few months later he could not refuse when his wife and son invited him to watch them being baptized. During the service, he listened carefully as the pastor described the need for salvation. His heart broke when he realized that his son had died without really knowing God, and that he, too, would die without hope.

During this time, only Barb and Freda had remained close. Hank and Gary had drifted apart. It was tragedy once again that brought focus back to the family. When Freda was diagnosed with breast cancer, those who believed prayed, and seeing no alternative, those who did not believe prayed as well. Freda's treatment began with chemotherapy and radiation. Shortly thereafter, she started to attend church with her family. Hank was overwhelmed not only with the loss of his father and his son, but also with his sister's condition. It was then that Hank realized he wanted the peace and comfort that could only be found in Jesus.

~ ~

One day, Hank answered his front door and found a young man standing there. Hank surmised from his dress and speech that he might be an African immigrant. Hank felt little desire to hear a sales pitch or a plea for a charitable donation to some unknown cause. But, as he attempted to brush the young man off with a "thanks but no thanks" and close the door, something caught his eye. A small, gold cross on a chain caught the sun and stood out against his dark skin.

With a compelling smile and an earnest look in his dark eyes he asked, "Would you pray for my family with me?"

At first Hank thought he had misheard the question and wondered how a stranger would have the nerve to ask such a thing. "I'm sorry," he said, "I'm not sure I heard you correctly."

"I have need of a friend to pray with me. I have read that where two or more are gathered we can ask what we want, and Jesus will answer our prayers. Is that not true?"

Hank was hurriedly wracking his brain, mentally searching for Scripture that might answer the question. "I cannot remember the chapter or verse. But yes, I think what you say is true. Unfortunately, I don't think it can be applied to every request."

"So you are a Christian then?" the young man asked. "You know what I am asking?"

"Will you come in? Maybe I can find the verse in the Bible. I think it is in the New Testament somewhere."

The young man came inside the house, but stood uncomfortably just inside the door. Hank offered him a seat in the living room while he retrieved Barb's Bible from their bedroom. The man sat as though ready to flee at a moment's notice.

"Would you like something to drink?" Hank asked, trying to set the young man at ease. "A soft drink or iced tea, perhaps?"

"Water would be nice."

As he was getting the man water, he said, "My name's Hank."

Taking the offered glass, the man smiled. "Thank you. I am called Gahiji."

Hank quickly perused the New Testament looking for key words. He stopped in Matthew at the words printed in red. "Again I say to you, that if two of you agree on earth about anything that they may ask, it shall be done for them by My Father who is in heaven. For where two or three have gathered together in My name, I am there in their midst. Matthew chapter 18, verses 19 and 20," he read.

Gahiji nodded. "Exactly as I remember it."

Hank felt a certain pride at having found the verses so easily. "What is the urgency that brings you to my door?" Hank asked, trying hard to phrase the question kindly while still amazed that they were sitting there together.

"I am here alone," Gahiji said. "I feel my brothers and sisters need God's help right now. They are in danger."

Hank was amused and curious at the same time. "Where are your brothers and sisters?"

"In Rwanda in a small village that is being attacked by those who follow the evil one." Gahiji seemed older now, more mature. "The effective prayer of a righteous man can accomplish much," he quoted, from memory.

Hank recognized the words and the context.

"Shall we pray for their protection?" Hank asked his guest before setting the Bible down.

A solemnity settled over the room, a quiet that muted the world around them as they bowed their heads together.

Gahiji began, "Father, our God in heaven, hear our prayers as

166

you always do. Your children are calling out for your protection from evil. We lift up our prayers with them, asking that you protect, comfort them, and give them peace."

Hank felt a little uncomfortable sitting alone with this stranger asking God's protection on behalf of someone he did not know. "God, I too ask you to bless and give safety to your children who are in danger. I pray that you will hear us, and comfort Gahiji as he fears for his brothers and sisters. Although he feels alone, give him the assurance that You are always with him. Amen."

Gahiji's smile was radiant as they lifted their heads and locked eyes for a moment. There seemed little more to say as Gahiji got to his feet and moved toward the door.

"Those who give peace, find peace," he said, stepping out of the doorway.

Hank closed the door behind him, then opened it again quickly with the intention of inviting Gahiji to join him for lunch. Gahiji was gone. In just seconds, he was nowhere in sight.

The five o'clock world news that evening told of militant attacks against Christian villagers in Africa. Hank was so glad that he had opened his heart to pray with Gahiji, build a cottage for his mother, and be there to comfort Gary. The truth of the matter was that by reaching out to them with prayer and love, Hank had found God was meeting the deepest needs in his life.

The Vicar

Undaunted by the rain, the vicar made his way quietly along the narrow, deserted street. An ancient streetlight would illuminate him from time to time in its golden glow, only to later give him back to the darkness. There were few out on the streets at this late hour. Most of the crowd from the pubs had already vanished into the night, leaving only a straggler or beggar here and there to occupy the darkened alcoves of the doorways. He may have done well to fear for his life had he not sensed the protecting hand of God.

At twenty-three, Harold McCreary was the youngest of the messengers that the prelate used as errand boys. It was not the work of the church that kept them busy, but rather personal matters that demanded discretion or secrecy. Of slight build and only medium height, there was little about Harold that one would count as remarkable until they looked into his translucent blue eyes. They were so striking that he became the center of attention at many gatherings.

The young women of the parish spoke of him with whispers and giggles, often finding their cheeks becoming flushed because of their unspoken thoughts. He had never encouraged a single one of them, but was not unaware of their interest. In fact, if the truth were told, he could easily picture himself taking them home for a special evening together. Occasionally it made him reflect on the course he might choose for his life. If he chose the life of a priest it would come with a vow of celibacy. He could not picture himself like the prelate, trying to serve God while juggling his vows and other passions. No, Harold would either choose to forgo the obvious pleasures of the world, or he would choose a profession that would let him enjoy them and still follow the tenants of his religion.

Inside a pocket, sewn into the lining of his outer coat, a sheaf of documents within a sealed envelope was safely protected from the rain. As he continued onward, Harold patted the coat, reassuring himself that it was still there. The narrow cobblestone street continued to wind between century-old shops and houses before beginning its descent toward the sea. In the distance, mast lights from ships at sea and those in the dockyard glimmered through the mist and darkness. At night, the harbor area was hardly a destination of choice for the upright. It was more likely a haven to many who used the cover of darkness in search of ill-gotten gain. There were a number of illicit pleasures within easy grasp – prostitutes, gambling, pubs, and potential riches gained from questionable transactions. The thought crossed his mind that he was being dispatched into the waiting jaws of the lion where he might be devoured and never seen again. Just as quickly, Daniel came to mind, and the story of the Lord's protection for His faithful one. He almost smiled at the speed with which God had responded to his moment of weakness. *No temptation has overtaken you but ... God ... will provide a way of escape*, was emblazoned across the blackboard of his mind.

He was dressed in the garments of the church, but not of those ordained to the priesthood. He was not among those the church referred to as "Father." It bothered Harold, when he let himself dwell on it, that the Word of God clearly said that only God was to be referred to as Father, and yet the church hierarchy took liberty to ignore it. He also found it difficult to believe that a priest could forgive a man's sins. But as they often reminded him, he was young and had much to learn about God and the church.

The night was quiet, unlike those on the mainland that were regularly interrupted by the sounds of explosions. At times the darkness was dispatched for a moment by the lights of exploding weapons of war somewhere in the distance. The smaller nations bordering Germany had fallen almost without notice to much of the world. The larger nations, like France and Spain, disbelieved the possibility of impending peril, preferring to reflect upon the glory days of centuries past. In London, a few scant miles away, parliament had met many times behind closed doors. Those having wisdom and insight had chosen not to underestimate the ambitions of Hitler and his forces. It was clear within the inner circles of power that the country must go to war.

Harold was now entering the waterfront area and was encouraged to see that it was being patrolled by armed members of the British military.

"Good evenin', Vicar," a young man with a rifle carelessly slung over his shoulder said, as he approached. "'Tis late to be out for a walk."

Harold nodded before handing the soldier his identification papers. "Indeed it is, but not too late to be about the church's business. I have a delivery for Commander Smythe."

"Right away. I'll take you to 'im."

Harold followed the lance corporal between several warehouses, and then on the boardwalk northward along the docks. Just ahead a dim light announced the presence of an occupied structure. Two raps on the door gained them entry into the cluttered office. Heavy, dark curtains had been installed across the windows to discourage uninvited visitors.

A tall, thin man with military bearing and a hawk-like nose approached Harold and stuck out his hand in greeting. "Vicar," he said, "I've been expecting you. You have something for me?"

"I do," Harold said, taking the sealed envelope from his coat and handing it to the commander.

"Please make yourself comfortable while I look this over," Commander Smythe invited. "I may have correspondence to return with you. Corporal, please see to the vicar's needs."

Harold took a seat in a straight-backed chair along the wall and waived off the corporal's attempt to bring him tea. He watched as the commander read and reread the prelate's letters, made notes, and circled items for later review.

Finally, Smythe looked up and grimly smiled while looking into Harold's blue eyes. "I'll be but a moment more," the commander apologized as if he were inconveniencing the young vicar. He sat at a worn desk and began to compose his response, taking several minutes and referring back to the documents numerous times. "I expect we'll be seeing you again," Smythe said, handing him a sealed envelope and offering his hand once more. "Corporal, kindly see this man back to the street."

In the days and weeks that followed, Harold made many more

trips like the first - always at night, always unaware of the contents of the correspondence he carried. Curious, yes, but not curious enough to open the documents with which he had been entrusted.

One night the commander let some information slip. He did not know of Harold's ignorance of the purpose of his mission. "One hundred twelve we've saved from the hands of that madman," the commander declared. "Tonight, if God is willing, a dozen more, or maybe two, may find their way across the channel to safety."

Harold considered carefully what he had just heard. "How many more are there?" he asked, not quite sure of who they were.

"You mean the Jews?" the commander asked. "Millions, I suppose, but far less are willing or able to leave their homeland. The Nazis have already killed many and are putting many more in prisons where they are left to die."

Harold was a quick study, picking up the implied but not completely defined mission. "Surely there are others like us who are willing to help," he said.

"Yes, many, all up and down the coast and even some countries are now offering refuge, but others are turning them away. The question remains, will they be safe here, or will we too fall to this madman?"

Within a few days of their conversation the answer to that question arrived in the form of German bombers making life uncertain for both the refugees and Britons alike. Air raid sirens became as natural as church bells. Death and destruction became commonplace on the besieged island.

Harold gathered his courage before asking for an audience with the bishop. He was not quite sure of what he intended to say. Apparently he was somewhat favored, or he would not have been selected for the rescue effort. His hope was that he would not be summarily dismissed by the powerful man. When he entered the chambers he was immediately stunned by their opulence. He felt and was made to feel even more insignificant by the manner in which he was greeted.

"Your Grace," Harold said. He then bowed slightly in a manner showing proper respect to the station. "Thank you for seeing me."

"Vicar Harold is it?" he asked, without looking up from the papers on his desk. "In what way may I be of service to you?"

Harold felt like laughing at the unusual way the bishop had spoken, but pleased that the man knew his name.

"If I may just ask you a question," Harold said.

The bishop looked up and then down his long nose through his glasses at the young man seated across his great desk. "What is it?" he finally asked.

"I'd be pleased to be used in a more hands-on way to facilitate the evacuation of those who are fleeing Germany and seeking asylum."

The bishop put down the papers, which had hereto occupied his time, and focused his stare at his subordinate. "By hands-on I assume you mean in some way other than carrying my correspondence to Commander Smythe and returning with his answers?"

"I am young, strong and willing," Harold said. "I thought I might be more valuable to the church out among the people we serve." Harold could see that the Bishop was carefully considering his response in light of the way he had presented his case.

"The Jewish people who refused to accept our glorious Savior and cried out to have Him put to death are now crying out to us in their

173

time of need," he remarked, apparently needing to vent his disdain for them. "We, of course, are commanded to love the least of these as ourselves."

Harold recognized the bishop's desire to preach rather than answer. "It is because of our love for Jesus that we aid them in their distress. I'll speak to the commander about the possibility of having you serve as a liaison between the refugees and the church."

"Thank you, your Grace," Harold said, standing to go.

"A question for you now," the bishop said. "How did you come to know about the church's involvement? Am I not able to trust correspondence to your care?"

Harold felt himself redden as he chose his words carefully. "You are. I have never compromised my integrity or betrayed your trust. It is God who chose to open my eyes to the truth," he said, finding himself surprised at his own answer.

"Very well," the bishop replied. "I'll let you know what we decide."

~ ~

The small fishing trawler bore the Swedish flag. Her carefully chosen crew spoke fluent Swedish as well as their native English. The boat's twin propellers had been replaced by a pair with greater pitch, trading power for speed. Still rigged with nets and fishing gear, the boat would have been ineffective in pulling them any distance. However, it was now able to top thirty-five knots on a favorable sea. The boat had a hidden shallow draft, which allowed it to run in five feet of water. The first week Vicar Harold McCreary spent much of his time leaning over the gunnel of the boat, feeding the fish the contents of his last meal. This week, however, God had provided a healing hand that allowed him to ignore the swaying boat and rolling waves. Just last evening a smaller boat had brought out through the pounding surf the twelve who were now huddled below deck. There were three men, four women, four children, and a nursing baby. Dutch Jews by birth who now had no place in their homeland. Harold had prayed for them and the crew, asking God's mercy and protection in waters patrolled by their enemy. Unlike these few, many of the Jews refused to believe the whispered tales that were heard in their homeland, believing only when it was too late to escape the hands of their captors. Indeed, it was unthinkable to a sane person that those who had been friends, neighbors and schoolmates could almost overnight become so filled with rage.

It was Commander Smythe's duty to coordinate pickup sites and provide air cover for his makeshift flotilla when they approached the English shores. The Royal Navy, for the most part, had its hands full patrolling the channel and engaging the war ships and submarines of the Germans. The Spitfires of the British Air Force proved effective in minimizing the German offensive against the small civilian boats in the channel. Between runs, Harold was charged with providing food and housing for the refugees. The church called upon its membership to volunteer as they were able. Harold, along with an interpreter, met with the refugees before dispersing them into private homes and spoke with them about the love of Jesus. Many, if not most, were unwilling to consider the New Testament promises, choosing instead to cling to the Talmudic precepts. However, from time to time some of the younger ones would listen with eager ears as Harold read and explained passages like Romans chapter 11, verse 24: "After all, if you were cut out of an olive tree that is wild by nature, and contrary to nature were grafted into a cultivated olive tree, how much more readily will these, the natural branches, be grafted into their own olive tree!" They could see both themselves and their Gentile friends in its teachings. Few, however, openly accepted Christ, knowing they would be outcasts and alone without the support of their kinsmen.

For two years Great Britain had encouraged the United States to join the war effort. It was true that through the Lend-Lease program the U.S. had been supplying Great Britain, Russia and China with war materials. But it was not until Japan attacked Pearl Harbor that Americans became galvanized enough to declare war and officially join in.

When the winter waters of the northern Atlantic became too treacherous for the smaller vessels, the pipeline began to dry up. This caused the refugees to seek asylum among their sympathizers on the mainland. In France, la resistance fighters were the only hope the refugees had for protection and provision. While refugees were not really among their priorities, there were some who were willing share from their scant supply of food. Everyone knew that at any time they might be discovered and hauled away to concentration camps. Stories abounded of resistance fighters who had been captured and tortured in attempts to ferret out the underground movement.

From time to time when necessity overcame caution, Harold

ventured from the safety of the vessel onto the soil controlled by the enemy. On one such adventure he had been guided to a vacant farmhouse. Its owners were either dead or conscripted into the service of the Third Reich. The house had missing windows, had been looted and partially burned. It stood askance on its stone foundation like a dead man with eyes staring into eternity. Carefully placed rubble concealed a doorway to an ancient stairwell leading to the cellar below. In that darkened, cramped space twenty Jews fearfully waited and prayed to be rescued. Harold and his compatriots came in answer to their prayer. Twenty was too large a number for the small boat to carry. Therefore it was decided that some would return to the waiting vessel while the others remained behind. Harold elected to be among those who stayed behind with the refugees. For six days and nights, marked only by the rising and setting of the sun, they hunkered down in the damp darkness together, hardly daring to speak and afraid to venture out. Late in the sixth night voices could be heard and the scraping of boots across the floor above as men searched the rubble for the entrance to their coffin-like abode. Harold could scarcely breathe, hearing his own heart beat in his chest as he waited.

After what seemed a lifetime, a cockney voice whispered, "Vicar, your ride has arrived."

Among those in his charge was a young, Jewish woman traveling alone. Her family had been taken away by the hated SS. She had eagerly listened to Harold during their time together in the cellar and came to believe that Jesus had brought the New Covenant with Israel into reality. In February 1942, at age twenty-six, Harold married Greta, a German-born Jew whom he helped immigrate into Britain. Ten days prior to Christmas, God blessed them with a daughter, Irene. Celebrating their first Christmas as a family, they attended Mass. In April of 1945, Harold surrendered his heart fully to Jesus and found a peace he had never known possible. In May of 1945, Harold's refugee work came to an end as Germany unconditionally surrendered and the entire world was on the pathway to peace.

Crisis

"Bring my golf clubs and a change of clothes by my office, and stop and grab a six-pack and bag of ice on the way," Brian said to his wife.

"You remember we have plans with Pastor Brad and his wife this evening, don't you."

"Yeah, yeah," he replied, irritation apparent in his voice. "Give them a call for us and tell them we'll have to make it another time, will you, hon? This guy I'm golfing with is a big client, a real mover and shaker. If I get in tight with him, who knows how many of his buddies will come along as clients."

Jane acquiesced to her new husband's demands, but not without making one final attempt. "This is the second time you've changed the plan with them at the last minute, Brian. Can't you schedule your golf game for another evening?"

"Got to strike while the iron's hot," Brian said, quoting some old sage from a previous generation.

Jane hung up the phone without further comment.

~ ~

It was past ten o'clock when Jane heard the garage door open and Brian's car pull in. Dinner had been in the refrigerator for nearly five hours and secretly she hoped it was ruined. This was not the vision she had held a year ago when he had asked her to marry him. She had admired his drive, his commitment to get ahead, and the integrity he seemed to have in his business. She had loved the way he always tried to put others first. But as it often goes, the person you know during courtship is different than the one you marry.

"I'm home," he said. "Sorry I'm so late."

Jane didn't get out of bed, but yelled from their bedroom, "Your dinner is in the fridge."

A few minutes later when he came into their bedroom, he attempted to cover up his mistakes with a false sense of happiness. Like a little kid, he was talking fast, hoping that the sheer volume of words would make up for the lack of thought that had gone into them. He  recounted everything from his precious golf match. He highlighted the birdie he got on the seventh hole and how his putter was "in the zone." The potential clients were a great bunch of guys, and he was certain that this round was going to lead to really big things. When he finally finished his spiel and crawled in beside her, she pretended to be asleep and did not respond to his touch. He smelled of alcohol and cigarette smoke. She let herself become angry, and felt justified in doing so. They finally drifted off to sleep, worlds apart.

Seven o'clock announced itself with an irritating buzz on the clock beside their bed. Normally Brian would have already been in and out of the shower and would have turned off the alarm before it rang. Jane was in the kitchen with a cup of coffee in her hand and the morning paper spread across the table.

She knew he was paying a price for his choices of the previous day and almost felt happy about his suffering. She felt convicted by the Holy Spirit, for it but was less than sincere when she asked for God's forgiveness.

It was a quarter to nine when Brian finally joined her in the kitchen. He was still in his sweats and looking like a child wanting to skip school.

"The office called," she said, trying not to smirk. "You need to call them back. Something about a closing that you missed for the Jones family."

Brian's face turned pale. "Oh, no! I forgot that their home closed today."

Jane felt sorry for him and badly about her feeling that he was being punished. "Would you like some breakfast," she offered. "I can fix you something while you shower."

Brian was already on the phone with his office, listening rather than talking as his broker unloaded on him.

"They had questions about the title company. They were wondering where you were. We tried to settle them down and get it closed over the phone. But in the end, Mr. Jones made it clear that neither he nor his family or friends would ever use our office again. Why didn't you answer your cell?"

181

Brian remembered he had left his cell phone in his golf bag in the car. "I spent the evening with new clients last night," he said. "I forgot to bring it in from the car when I got home."

"I'll expect you in my office as soon as you get in," the broker said.

Brian had enjoyed "golden boy" status in the realty office. It seemed that every decision he made literally turned to gold. His closings and earnings were nearly double that of his more seasoned peers, and with it the number of referrals and listings kept pace.

When he and Jane had married, he jumped into the business with both feet. His goal was to provide for her in a handsome fashion. He of course knew that meant sacrifice and time away from home. That was not what she had envisioned for their lives when they stood at the altar. What she did know was that they lived well in a new home that was the envy of her friends. What she hoped for was that things would normalize and at some point they could enjoy their lives and begin a family.

Unfortunately, the momentum of each sale spawned more activity, more money, and higher goals that demanded more time to accomplish. From Jane's point of view he had put her and their marriage on the back burner, with money and prestige taking precedence over both. What she wanted back was the man she thought she had married. What he wanted was an understanding wife who would accept what he viewed as a short-term inconvenience in exchange for long-term security and success.

~ ~

It was not the first time Pastor Brad had heard a version of this story, and he knew it would certainly not be the last. He had seen the signs of their impending marital distress. He offered advice, which they had both ignored in order to pursue their individual goals. He knew that their individual goals were the problem. When the "we" became "me" in their marriage, and the "He," as in God, began to be replaced by things, it did not take long before the marriage began to fall apart. As he prepared for a counseling session with the young couple, he wondered how he would present his case this time.

When he performed their marriage, he had no sense of division or conflict. They seemed committed to Jesus and to one another. Now, several months later, their prosperity was threatening to destroy their marriage. The fact that a scheduled social time together had failed three times should have alerted him to the potential trouble.

Before they arrived, he looked to God in prayer, asking that the Holy Spirit would soften their hearts during the session. He would repeat the same prayer again when they arrived, hoping they too would invite God to help them in their decisions. He knew Satan would likely try to make defensive and closed to each other's needs.

~ ~

Brian came unwillingly, displaying in his posture his resolve to deny responsibility. Jane sat uncomfortably beside him, looking desperate and unhappy. It did not go unnoticed by Brad that they arrived separately.

"So," Pastor Brad began, "here we are, already at a place that I had hoped we would never be." He struggled to make eye contact as neither seemed willing to let him into their private thoughts. "Please look at me," he said firmly but gently, watching as each looked up at him. He held their gaze for a moment and said, "Now please look at each other."

Tears rimmed Jane's eyes as she looked at the man she loved. Brian's eyes were filled with pain and disappointment as he observed her tears.

He let the moment ferment for several seconds before he continued. "Let us join hands and ask our Lord and Savior for His comfort and peace."

Brad noted how they reached out to each other, tentatively at first, then with more and more resolve and commitment. He let them feel the warmth of union for a few seconds before he began to pray. As they prayed, Jane began to cry gently. As they continued, she gave way to sobs of pain. She held on desperately to Brian's hand, unwilling to let it go. Brian too had tears running down his cheeks.

Finally, as the prayer ended, the three raised their heads and eyes without speaking. Feeling the presence of the Lord in the room, Brad let the moment last a few more seconds.

"Please consider that all good things come from God...meaning *all* good things. We have nothing except what God has given us," he said. "Principal among those good things is His love."

Both nodded.

"God loved you first so that you could learn and understand love. He gave it to you unconditionally, hoping you'd receive it and give it back to Him and to His children. Jesus described this in the most important commandments. They are found in Matthew chapter 22, verses 35 through 40. Do you understand this?"

Both Brian and Jane nodded without speaking.

"It goes right along with the commandment that we are to have no other gods but the one true God," he continued. "When we take our eyes off God and let them rest on anything else for a time, we become tempted to let it become our god. But if we maintain our focus on God, then we are able to make good decisions. We cannot fix what is broken. Only God can do that. But we need to return to Him and ask, and He promises to help us."

They were both looking at him with tear-stained cheeks.

Pastor Brad smiled. "When you return to your first love, He will help you return to each other. Let the "I" and "me" in your lives be replaced with "He."

~ ~

These things should be self-evident to followers of Jesus, but they seldom are. We often need a reminder to guide us back when we have taken our eyes off the prize.

Gratitude

The click, click, click of the drag sounded like zzzzs as the big fish stripped line off the old, level wind reel. The sound took him back to a time when he stood with his grandpa in this very stream. Now he was a  grandpa. But his grandkids had left town years ago searching for their place in this world. He couldn't believe how quickly the years had passed. Of course, when he had been in the stream with his grandpa, he heard people say such things and passed them off as "stupid things that old people say." Now here he was living it out like it had happened just a moment ago.

The fish found its head and was using the force of the current against his body to add power to his run. Grant's thumb came down slowly, gently against the line on the spinning drum, adding tension until it came to a halt. Like a pole-vaulter, the fish used the tension of the pole and stretch of the line combined with his strength to break free of the water's hold as he leapt into the air. He was beautiful. The sun's rays caught the spectrum of color from his broad scaled side and reflected the colors of the rainbow.

This is as good as it gets, Grant thought, wishing for an audience as he stood on the bank of his favorite stream. This memory shared with friends, his kids, and or grandkids, would have been the ultimate adventure. Grant wondered what kind of special memories would be available for his grandchildren when they reached his age. Their world didn't seem to leave much space for times like this.

The fish shook its head back and forth in the air. The fly showed plainly in the gristle of its upper lip. *Keep the line taut*, came a voice from the past that filled his head with wise council. The words of his grandfather echoed from a half dozen decades before when he was just a boy.

The water washed the sand and small stones out from under the soles of his boots, causing his footing to change and constantly forcing him to adapt or fall. It became evident that the force of the water and the size of his adversary made it crucial that he follow the fish rather than try and hold it. Grant moved downstream slowly and carefully, keeping tension on the pole and tiring the fish. The fish broke water again, this time from a shallow riffle near a gravel bar on the right side of the stream.

Grant maintained his position on the left side, working the reel and collecting line to prevent opportunity to slip the hook. A brown blur in his peripheral vision caught his attention, causing him to move his focus off the fish. He guessed it was a sow, about two or three years old and maybe 175 pounds, a good size for a black bear. She made it across the fifty-foot width of the gravel bar from the tree line in just seconds and had his prize in her mouth before he could raise a cry. Not that it would have made a difference anyway, as he was not armed and a shout would not have deterred her.

A quick jerk loosened the marabou jig, saving his line and drift rig. As he watched, he reeled in the line. The bear retreated a few yards and began to eat its catch. *You are welcome*, he silently said to the bear. *Enjoy your meal.* The day was over for Grant, so he made it to the bank and crawled from the water. It had been a good one. In fact, better than most. There were four smaller fish in his creel, more than enough for supper. He wondered now if he'd have kept the big rainbow anyway. *Probably not*, he thought.

He walked slowly and painfully as he made his way over rocks and between brush and willows that seemed to be reaching out toward him. The rush of the water was always a comfort to him, as was the stillness which it interrupted. The stream's cold water had relieved the pain of arthritis in his joints, but now it was returning with a vengeance. Every step brought pain. When he considered his choices, he shrugged it off and attempted to put it out of his mind. He was going to die. *We all do*, he thought, which left him only the choice of how to spend his time until it came. But now, there was little about the sunrise that sparked his interest. The challenge of the outdoors was to only thing that gave him joy or any desire to leave the familiarity of his home.

Tyke must have caught his scent as he yelped a greeting to his master from the bed of the old, green pickup. Tyke was more crippled than his master, and older too if you are to believe the seven times thing about dogs. They had gotten him as a pup fourteen years ago. He was nearly blind, had dysplasia in both hips, and was wracked with arthritis. Grant had to gently lift him into the pickup, and would lift him out again at home.

Grant smiled back. "We got supper."

The dog wagged his tail. Grant had found that one of the keys to life was gratitude…to be grateful and contented with what you have. It was a lesson he had learned from his friend, the apostle Paul, years ago when he and his wife had attended church regularly and gotten deeply involved in Bible study. It had been especially hard to feel any gratitude at all when he lost Mary. The pain had overwhelmed and crippled his spirit for a time, but gradually the sweet memories returned and became his anchor. He began to be thankful for them and grateful for those years they had shared. Every day brings a host of things to be thankful for, if we reflect on the One who loves us and the many blessings He brings into our lives. Grant found that when he stopped dwelling on the sorrows of yesterday he could still enjoy his daily routines and activities. A prime example had been the nice rainbow he had lost, and the thrill of watching the black bear. Gratitude begins when one accepts neither the glass is half full nor the glass is half empty message, but embraces the fact that when we walk with God, a bright future always lies ahead.

The old Chevy turned over slowly, grinding painfully before it caught. Grant thanked the Lord as he ground it into gear and headed down the trail toward the gravel road. If it hadn't started it would have been a serious problem. No one lived within ten miles. The fact that no one knew where he was, or would miss him if he failed to return home, never concerned him. He had a thermos of coffee, a coat, matches, four nice fish, and Tyke. What more could a man want? His concern was not for himself, but for Tyke. If he passed on first and it happened at his house, he knew that his neighbors would care for Tyke. But if it happened out here it would be a real problem. Tyke sniffed the creel as he settled into the front seat beside Grant and seemed to smile.

~ ~

Millbrook no longer sported a brook or a mill, which had been its claim to fame at the turn of the century. The little stream had been tilled and ran underground now, no longer furnishing water for the millpond that had been filled in when the mill had closed and been disassembled. What was left was a nice place to live in retirement, but one that held no future for the children. They moved on to the big cities chasing work and living life at a frantic pace, which left little room for reflection and restoration. Fifteen miles from the interstate and without commerce, Millbrook lived on at a much slower pace, and like its dwindling population, endured simply because it could. The businesses had consolidated as the population which supported them had moved on, leaving behind a mercantile with a pair of gas pumps and a post office. The merc sold clothing, household products, a few farming supplies, food and over-the-counter drugs, much like the old-time country store of the 50s.

Grant laughed every time he passed the place thinking about its owners, a pair of elderly twin sisters whose parents had chosen to name them Mercy and Grace…back in the day when it was considered to be in good taste. Neither had ever married, living in Millbrook since childhood and taking over ownership from their parents upon their deaths. In older times the mercantile was more of a combination hardware and feed store than a quick mart, catering to animal needs, horseshoes, shovels, axes, pitchforks and tack.

He reigned in the old Chevy and parked in front of the outdated gas pumps. He didn't need gas, but felt obliged to buy something, and keeping the tank full was just good planning. When he paid for the overpriced fuel he also purchased two hand-dipped, single-scoop cones: one chocolate for him and the other vanilla for Tyke. The two old friends sat together enjoying the quickly setting sun and their cold, creamy treats before driving the three blocks home. Grant gently lifted his friend from the seat and placed him on the front lawn. Tyke sniffed around a little before doing his business in the grass. Together they entered the old house through the rear door, and Grant turned on the kitchen light.

Evening Grant, came the voice from the doorway of the dimly lit living room. *You're a little late getting home tonight.*

Grant answered without thinking. "Stopped to gas up and have an ice cream with my friend 'fore coming home."

How did you do? he was asked through the darkness.

"Brought home four." Grant took the fish from the creel and put them on the cutting board. "Lost a big 'un to a bear."

A bear? the voice queried. *How'd that come about?*

Grant smiled, reliving the incident. "An ol' sow saw him jump and wanted dinner worse than me, I 'spect."

A rich laugh came from the shadows. *You fixin' to fry 'em up for supper then?*

"I am that," Grant answered. "I wish you could enjoy them with ol' Tyke and me. They're good and fresh, pink meat. I 'spect I'll roll 'em

191

in flour with salt and pepper, then fry 'em crisp like Mary used to. Would you like to join me?"

That's a tempting offer old friend. Thank you. There was a time when I could have enjoyed sup with you like I did when we stopped and shared a meal with Brother Abraham before going on to Sodom.

"I remember reading about that," Grant said. "That's when Sarah found out she was having a child, as I recall." Grant laughed, putting himself in the same circumstance. "I think Mary and I'd have had a hard time believing it ourselves if you had come to tell us that."

The visitor laughed. *Your faith ebbs and flows like that stream you were fishing today, Grant. Sometimes the world hides reality from you, and sometimes reality shows the world to you.*

Grant pondered what he had heard. "Don't 'spect you can smell, can you?" he asked, as the fish began to pop in the oil of the cast iron skillet, filling the air with a pleasing aroma.

I can't unless I come in the flesh, he answered. *I have come with some good news to share with you.*

"And what might that be?"

You will be with Mary again soon.

"Praise God!"

Indeed.

As Grant bowed his head, old Tyke seemed to do so as well. Grant asked the Lord to bless the bounty they were about to share. It seemed important to him that he would express his gratitude for these fish that had been especially provided for him.

Grant took his first bite, handed some to Tyke, and then looked toward where his visitor stood. "I wish I could share with you. They're mighty tasty."

His second bite contained a fine bone. He tried to swallow, but it caught in his throat and caused him to cough. As the coughing became acute and the lack of oxygen severe, the strain caused an aortic aneurysm to burst near his heart. In seconds Grant was where he wanted to be, with Mary welcoming him with open arms, Jesus smiling, and the entire host declaring God's glory.

Out of Our Element

The place was foreign to him. He struggled to breathe, and efforts to find oxygen in the strange atmosphere were futile. He lay in the rocks beside the cool water of the small lake. His efforts grew feeble until at last he found release in death.

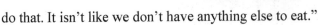

"Throw it back," his sister said with concern in her young voice.

"Too late," Andy answered, "he's already dead. Now we'll have to eat him."

"I hate it when you do that. It isn't like we don't have anything else to eat."

Andy had nine like it already on the stringer. They soon picked up their poles and headed home. *Mom will be pleased with today's catch, and we'll enjoy a nice meal of rainbow trout,* he thought. His mother would take the small fish after he had cleaned them, roll them in seasoned flour and fry them in her big, black, cast iron skillet. Being small, the fish would be cooked until crisp and often even the bones would be eaten.

Andy loved to fish, and at age twelve he was quite an accomplished fisherman. He had picked up the basics from his father and spent most of his spare time refining his technique. He knew the small lake like the back of his hand, including which little coves often harbored his prey. He had hardly ever been skunked and forced to return home without a catch. His sister, Olivia, was only ten. Like him, she loved the outdoors and the time they spent together. She did not, however, feel the need to keep the beautifully colored fish, and often chose to let them go.

His parents did not feel that the little lake posed much of a drowning hazard and thus gave the children free reign to fish it whenever they desired. As the small freezer compartment of their refrigerator began to fill up, Andy's father would impose a minimum size to slow down their harvest.

Their acreage was near the outskirts of the small town of Hill City, Idaho. It was in an open valley sandwiched by mountains to the northwest and southeast. The valley farms raised grain and alfalfa mostly as feed for their cattle. A rail line ran the length of the valley and as far north as the mining towns in the Wood River Valley before traveling south and west to Boise and on to the West Coast. Just north and over the mountains was the site of a great gold discovery in the century before. Many, like their father, continued to search for the undiscovered gold, which might still lay hidden beneath the soil.

Like the prospectors of a dozen decades before, Norm knew that just over one more hill, in one more shovel full of dirt, or beneath one more rock, the fortune he sought was waiting for him. But as he searched for the elusive treasure, he left his wife and family to learn to live without him. Joining his family for church on Sunday mornings was the exception rather than the rule. Nell, Andy and Olivia were well known and well accepted in the small community, while Norm often complained that they treated him like an outsider. Like an addict, Norm always seemed to find just enough gold to keep him coming back – just enough to draw him into the mountains to search for more.

A short drive down the dirt road, the town of Fairfield collected a more diverse and larger population. It was a scheduled stop for the train to pick up and empty livestock, passengers and manufactured goods from Salt Lake City and points east. Ore from the few remaining mines was loaded and transported to the nearest smelter. In the predominantly rural states out West, the 1950s were a unique mixture of animal labor and mechanization.

In the absence of a second vehicle, Norm still used his saddle horse and pack mules to traverse the rough terrain that led away from their home. It seemed as if every mountain or valley held the promise of certain reward. He was a throw back from the century before, in both manner and disposition. Nell often wondered if he had been born at the wrong time in history.

"Two weeks," he said, tying the last of his provisions on an old, red mule. "I've got a real good feeling about this."

Nell and the children just nodded, having heard the same words many times before.

"There's dried apples, apricots and fresh bread in the side bag. I've wrapped the jars of canned goods in flour sacks so they won't get broken," Nell said, pointing to the gunny that hung on his mare behind the saddle.

"Thanks," Norm said, as he turned toward her. "I'll miss you all. Andy, take care of the women."

Andy nodded. "I will, Father," he said, dutifully. "And you be careful."

Andy surprised himself when he said the last sentence, wondering where the admonition had come from. He could not remember a previous time when he had added such a caveat to his goodbye. The three stood watching until the horse, its rider, and the mule disappeared into the background of sagebrush and juniper that led into the adjacent mountains.

Some chores varied with the season and others were just a natural part of life in the circumstance in which the family lived. Although they now had electricity and running water inside the house, they still utilized the wood stove for heating and cooking. This of course required an ample supply of split wood and kindling. Their cow and other critters, as they were called, found forage in season but relied upon the family to supplement water and feed when the stream dried up or became frozen. The milk cow had this year's calf by her side.

Andy inherited the milking chore from his father when it became evident that Norm would be away more often than home. He would tuck his blond hair against her flank and strip the last drop from her teats morning and night. When he first learned to milk, it required several periods of rest to get through the ordeal. His young hands ached from the unfamiliar exercise. His mother could do it as well, and did so when necessary, but it was considered man's work, so Andy or his father shouldered most of the load. Olivia helped her mother feed the chickens, gather the eggs, and take care of the cats and dogs. The division of labor seemed to work well in spite of Norm's lack of supervision.

Nell hoped Norm would keep his pledge to return in two weeks, but feared that fall would once again arrive without them having the chance to haul in the necessary firewood from the surrounding hills. He had been known to remain out for long stretches when the need of a man with an ax and saw was most pressing. She had never questioned his discipline, but was concerned about his priorities.

Early August arrived with most of the early garden vegetables safely in the root cellar or in canning jars. Very little remained to be done except to store the carrots, squash and potatoes. Andy always marveled at how his mother could serve fresh tasting vegetables when the weather outside was hovering at zero and the snow had drifted higher than their clothesline.

Norm and Nell had married in 1946. Andy was born a few months later. It was hardly a surprise to the families who had disapproved of the returning veteran who talked coarsely and drank liberally. "A dreamer and a wanderer," Nell's grandmother had said. "Not one who will settle down, get a job, and raise a family." *She had been right in most of her critical appraisal*, Nell thought to herself, except that they were raising a family and proud of the children. Norm had worked at the mill, for a time, but found it hard to take orders. He had also worked with a logging crew, but questioned the judgment of his foremen. He seemed to be of the opinion that others lacked his unique ability to see the easiest ways to accomplish their tasks and made it known to them. They in turn found others more willing to be led.

Norm had been gone for seventeen days, and school was about to begin. With the cold fall and winter only a whisper away, they were running low on firewood. Nell drove into town with the children and stopped at the mill where she found she could get a load of "buckskins" hauled out to the house for forty dollars. Buckskins were trees that had died while still standing and had lost most of their bark before being felled for firewood. She remembered how Norm had coveted the few they had found as though they were a prize. She was conflicted, knowing that Norm still held animosity for the mill and its owners, but mindful of the need to guarantee adequate wood for heating. In the end, she thanked them, said she would make a decision later in the week, and left saying a little prayer on the drive home. A little over a hundred dollars still remained in her mother's sugar bowl, the result of her summer sales of jams and jellies.

When he had been gone nearly three weeks, the county sheriff paid a visit. Behind his old pickup was a stock trailer with the red mule aboard, but no sign of either Norm or his mare.

"One of the boys from the logging crew found him wandering," he announced. "He recognized him and brought him back to town."

Andy took the mule to the barn and fed it.

Tears welled up in Nell's eyes as she asked, "But no sign of Norm?"

"I am afraid not," he answered gently. "They did not spend a lot of time looking since they were on the job. Do you have any idea where he may have gone?"

"No," Nell answered. "He talks about each mountain, rock slide, and stream like they are his friends, like we should know them too, but of course we do not."

The large man frowned, shaking his head as he considered the possibilities.

"Owens Creek," she said suddenly. "I remember him talking about Owens Creek."

The sheriff's face brightened. "That'll give us a place to start," he said. "I'll get some volunteers to go out with me in the morning. I'll let you know what we find."

"Sheriff, could we ask you for a favor?"

"Sure, what do you need?"

"First, would you stop and tell the pastor about our situation, and ask him to pray for Norm? Then, if you would, tell Rob at the mill that we will take the load of buckskin logs we talked about. I'd appreciate it."

He nodded. "Be pleased to. Try not to worry. He's probably just got turned around and is waitin' for someone to find him."

Andy came back to the house. "Where's Dad?" he asked.

Nell told him the story the sheriff told her, emphasizing his last remarks. She asked the children to pray with her. When they said amen, all three had tears lining their cheeks and fear in their hearts.

Two days later a crew of men from the mill showed up with a load of wood. They had blocked and split it on their own time. They refused her attempts to pay the forty dollars, saying only that it was their gift. They each accepted a hug and several jars of blackberry preserves before leaving for their homes.

A knock on the door interrupted dinner. The sheriff and his wife stood on the porch with a basket of food. Sadness reflected in their eyes.

"Please come in," Nell said apprehensively.

They entered and took a seat in the living room, and the children joined them.

"We found his horse at the bottom of Owens Creek. It had a broken neck. It appears it lost its footing on the trail above and fell. We found no sign of Norm."

"So," Olivia said hopefully, "that means he's all right."

The sheriff looked at the others, took a breath, and said, "We hope so, but we won't be sure until we find him. We'll be going back out in the morning with the dogs."

Andy felt like he'd swallowed a rock. Heaviness settled over him, and a desperate hopelessness began to fill his mind. He could picture his father lying dead or alone and badly injured.

"I'll come with you," Andy said with more authority than he felt.

"No, son," the sheriff said gently but firmly. "I can't allow that. The country is too rough, and we can't take time to worry about you getting hurt. Besides, your family needs you here with them."

Andy knew he was right and knew that he would be of little use if he were to go. He nodded and said, "You are right. Dad told me to take care of the women."

Both pride and pain shone in Nell's eyes as she held her children close.

"We are all praying for you," the sheriff's wife said. "The whole church is praying."

Two nights later, just before the children headed off to bed, a knock on the door made everyone's heart skip a beat. Again it was the sheriff. This time he was skirted by several of his deputies. All were showing the strain of the day in their faces.

He hesitated a moment before speaking. "We found him, and he's alive. But, he has been badly injured."

"Where is he?" Nell asked. "When can we see him?"

"He's with the doc in town. They're making arrangements to get him to the VA hospital in Boise. It would probably be better if you wait until morning, after he's had a chance to rest."

Neither Nell nor the children wanted to wait, but the tone of the sheriff's voice had a warning hidden somewhere within.

Nell nodded, hugged both children close, and said, "Thank you. Thank you all, and thank God."

Over the next few days the story of Norm's ordeal came out bit by bit as if it were both physically and mentally painful to tell. Luckily when the mare lost her footing, Norm had let go of the mule's lead rope, which kept the mule from falling down the steep hillside. If he had not let go, both animals may have been involved and several days would have passed before anyone would have taken up a search. The horse had been killed in the fall. Norm had fractured both legs and his pelvis, which prevented him from standing or walking. He was able to drag himself to his mining tunnel where he endured the cold and nursed his injuries until help finally arrived. Miraculously the gunny and its contents survived without incident. As he lay alone and helpless in the shelter of the tunnel, Norm survived for seven days on the scant rations Nell had put together.

Weeks later when he was well enough to complain, he said that the trip over the dirt road from Fairfield to Boise hurt more than the fall down the hill. The hospital kept him for six weeks and sent him home in the middle of the winter to a family eager to be reunited. Norm said to anyone who would listen that through this ordeal God had used extreme measures to gain his attention and bring him to a newfound faith.

Fissure I

A small hairline crack, barely visible to the naked eye, appeared in the polished surface of the exterior housing. A stress crack, no doubt, caused by the extremes of temperature and the incalculable pressures it had endured. But it was not the human eye that had discovered it; it was the probing eyes of the magnified cameras that went over the surface millimeter by millimeter after each mission. Perfection was impossible. There were always defects to be discovered, analyzed by the computer, and then referred to men of science for further evaluation. If the computer had the final say, any flaw or imperfection would have been viewed as critical and prevented the next mission. With the exception of the *Challenger* and *Columbia* disasters, man's judgment had been proven to be adequate.

There was great debate as to whether the computer should complement or supersede man's judgment. Unfortunately man's judgment was determined to have preeminence in this massive endeavor. There was pressure from without that called them to be fiscally responsible with the taxpayers' money. To many observers that was a joke. Congressional committees could always afford what they wanted regardless of the funding issues. They may cut funding to Social Security or domestic needs, but they would never cut back when trying to buy their enemy's friendship, or unlock the secrets of God's universe.

This massive expenditure, very much like the Mercury, Gemini and Apollo programs, appealed to man's need for discovery and exploration. But what truly had been gained by walking on the moon? Yes, the United States' defense system had gained a clear military advantage in space, but other than that, the "single step for mankind" seemed to have little impact on our everyday lives. The focus quickly changed to exploring the vast unknown regions of the galaxies, but no one could really explain why. One might imagine that they are hoping to find life in some distant place so they could support their hypothesis that life appears out of nothing. The more science tried to discredit God, digging ever deeper into the vast array of stars with its probing telescopic eyes, the more it confirmed His existence.

~ ~

The date is January 15, 2024. The world did not end on December 22, 2012, as the Mayans prophesied, nor will it until the day and hour prescribed by God. The massive ship, *Abble I,* stands silent, attached by its umbilical beside the tower that provides it sustenance. The countdown is still days and hours away as systems checks and tests are performed. Faceless men in various shades of sage-green jump suits, color coded to indicate their various departments, and others in gray, white, blue and tan attire focus on their fields of expertise.

It seems that God allows man to advance his knowledge in spurts. Mankind moves ever forward in his search to rebuild the Tower of Babel. The massive ship had flown only twice before - once in subspace, and the other into the vacuum of outer space toward the moon at sublight speed. This flight is designed to propel man at light speed, challenging the laws of both time and space, possibly even opening the door to future time travel.

More and more unanswered questions seemed to surface as the launch neared. If they achieve light speed, will there be a relationship to time as we measure it? Will their bodies physically move forward or backward in time, actually aging or becoming younger? It could be reasoned that, if they moved toward the suspected point of creation, that time would be of yet unknown future events. It was stuff of which sci-fi is made. Conjecture about parallel universes, dual identities in different ones, and finding other species on distant worlds dominated the world's conversations. Vast sums of money were to be gained or lost over bets made supporting one position or another.

~ ~

"I wonder if God is laughing or crying as He looks at mankind and watches him reach for the stars," Derek said. "All over the world nations are letting their young and old starve in the streets as they drain their economies to send their representatives on this mad adventure."

"We've got to be a disappointment to Him," Sheila answered. "I'm sure that if He hadn't already known it would happen, He'd be saddened."

205

They were lying on their backs in the Arizona desert with an unobstructed view of God's creation. The blackness of the night showcased the vast array of stars looking down on them. The crisp night air of the high desert hovered just above freezing, making their down-filled bags a necessity. They saw the vapor of their breath when they spoke. Their tent stood nearby and would serve to protect them against inclement weather and small animals when they chose to move inside.

"I'm pregnant," she said, without preliminary discussion.

"I know. You told me," he answered, smiling.

"I mean now that I'm pregnant, things are different for me," she clarified.

"Obviously," he answered, laughing. He thought about the little pouch that seemed to encompass her navel.

"You know what I mean," she said, trying to sound disgusted. "I have to look at things differently now."

"What things? Does another life really change what you believe?"

"I feel like I should be more responsible, plan ahead, and put more thought into my choices."

"And what makes that different? You have always been levelheaded, used common sense, tried to make good decisions. Was marrying me a good decision? If you were deciding now with a bun in the oven, would I be in or out?"

"Dummy," she said sweetly, "if I hadn't married you, there'd be no bun in the oven, as you so crudely put it."

"Why are we here?" he asked suddenly.

"You wanted …," she began to answer.

"No, I mean why are we here on the Earth? Why were we created?"

"The Bible says ..."

"I know what the Bible says," he said, interrupting her again. "Why do you think we are here?"

Sheila could almost see him smiling. "To bring God glory," she said with conviction.

"I agree. How can we do that?"

"We can let Him live though us every minute of our lives."

"Amen. Do you think we are doing that?"

"You mean right now? This very minute?"

"You were the one who said every minute of our lives," he answered, laughing. "What does every minute mean to you?"

"Almost every minute, I mean. We have to have time for ourselves."

"Really?" he said questioningly. "How do we do that? Do we put God in the other room and lock the door while we have some fun?"

"Stop it!" she said. "You know how I hate it when you do that."

"Do what?"

"Suck me into one of your discussions where I always say the wrong thing."

"Back to my question. Do you think we are letting Him live through our lives and bringing Him glory?"

"Okay, preacher," she said, looking at him in the moonlight, "let's count the positives first. The negatives of our sinful flesh speak for themselves. We have Jesus as our Savior. We have eternal life guaranteed with Him. We have asked and continue to ask forgiveness for sin. We believe in His death and resurrection and claim His promises. Did I miss anything?"

"Not a thing, except the hard part, continuing daily to place our faith and trust in Him."

"I do that. Don't you?"

"I try," he said. "But we often hedge our bets in this world."

"Give me an example," she said sounding irritated.

"We have the same trouble fully trusting God as Israel did after God parted the Red Sea for them. We always want one more proof. Why do you suppose God only gave them enough manna for a single day?"

"So they could learn to depend on Him," she said with conviction.

"Right! And what was the first thing some tried to do?"

"Save some for the next day."

"Because some of them had doubts. They judged God the way they judged man as unfaithful or unable to keep promises. They tried to cover their bases."

"Do we do that?"

"Yes!" he said emphatically. "And then we justify it by saying God expects us to be good stewards and use good judgment."

"Like?" Sheila asked.

"Simple things, really. I really don't know which show a lack of faith and which reveal good planning. Health insurance, door locks, retirement funds, life insurance, immunizations, even a spare tire on our car, could be viewed as questioning God's ability to provide."

"So you are saying we should live by blind faith and not use common sense?" she asked raising her voice a bit.

"Not at all. I am saying that hedging our bets is a slippery slope that we need to carefully consider. When we contemplate such things, we are back to a question. Did God create it? Or did God allow it? If we view medical science as a gift from God, then it makes perfect sense to go to a hospital. But if we believe that man is our only hope for our physical health, then we are replacing God. If we believe that God can heal us apart from medical science, would we be questioning His ability to meet our need when we pay for health insurance and seek out a doctor? It all begins with what we believe about God and His ways of working in our lives."

"When we get home, you need to use this in one of your sermons. Our congregation will really love that." she said sarcastically.

~ ~

On the morning of the second day they went looking for the small cluster of buildings that made up the village. Since ancient times this area had been the home of the Pueblos who had lived in the cliffs of the encircling mountains nearby.

This was Derek's second visit to the village, the first having been while still apprenticing as a pastor. He knew they were in the right area, but when the road came to a fork he was unsure of which of the three roads they needed to take. They parked the Jeep and did a little searching on foot.

By noon they had made their way down the rocky terrain and were following the single-track road into the horseshoe. If Derek had remembered the way, they would have arrived in their Jeep two hours earlier and been a little less weary.

A squat, heavy-featured man, with flecks of white beginning to show in his jet-black hair, welcomed them with a grin. Around him were crowded a motley assortment of young and old, curious and excited to have visitors. Two dozen shacks, covered with rusting tin roofs and wrapped in weathered wooden siding, had replaced the caves of their ancestors. A single structure stood out from the rest, both in size and location. It stood in the center of several acres, with the other buildings arranged around it as if protecting it from assault.

Little had changed since his visit three years ago except the look of expectancy on the faces of his hosts. Of the thirty-five or so that attended Pastor Brown's service, three children had accepted the Lord. They and their families had greatly anticipated Derek's visit.

"Welcome friends," chief Thom said in a deep baritone voice that echoed off the walls. The greeting was repeated three dozen times by those around them. It was easy to see from the dark, heavy features of the men and women that their race remained pure and unpolluted by the outside world. When Derek had first seen them, he thought of the Aborigines of Australia who seemed to look unchanged for thousands of years.

"Thank you," Derek said. He motioned with his hand toward Sheila and said, "Sheila, my wife."

The crowd voiced their welcome.

"You did not drive?" the chief asked. He knew it was 150 miles to the nearest town.

"We did, but left the Jeep at the three forks. I feared I would take the wrong one and get lost."

Thom repeated the story in his own language, which brought much laughter.

"But yet you could find us when walking?"

"With God's help," he said, "we walked only a short way."

When Thom repeated Derek's account, there were smiles and more laughter. "Ten miles from three forks," he said. "You did well, your woman with child."

Both Sheila and Derek wanted to ask how Thom would know such a thing, as she was only in the second month. Instead they exchanged looks and remained silent. They were taken to one of the homes whose occupants had already been evacuated to another location. They were then given time to wash up and change their clothes. When they stepped out into the sunlight, it was blinding. The ground radiated heat as though the little, boxed canyon harbored fire under its sandy surface. Derek could only imagine the summertime temperatures in this stone furnace.

"We eat?" Thom said, to the pair as much a question as an invitation.

When they entered the meeting hall, everyone was already

quietly seated with heads bowed. Derek felt like the pope as he thanked God for the food before the assembled crowd. As they ate, both Derek and Sheila could taste the influence of the Mexican and Indian cultures brought together long ago.

After they finished eating, Thom suggested he might retrieve their vehicle. Derek elected to ride along, wanting to memorize his return path while Sheila stayed behind and rested. Just over an hour later they returned and began unloading the vehicle. Derek's church had provided several dozen New Living Translation Bibles. In addition, there were several boxes of food, toys, clothing and gifts. As they lined up, Sheila disbursed the items. Clothing, especially hats, seemed to be coveted by the men and cookware by the women.

Before leaving home, Derek had pondered what subject he might teach, waiting on the Holy Spirit for inspiration. When none had been revealed, he decided to combine the Christmas story with the resurrection. He presented them as bookends to the most amazing life ever lived. He and Sheila had highlighted and bookmarked both stories in each of the Bibles that were handed out. Sheila brought many visual aids, pictures and drawings from her youth group, and sat them on a table in the front. As he began to tell the familiar story, she would point to the appropriate pictures, often receiving nods and smiles for her trouble. As the sun was setting outside, Jesus had just tipped over the tables of the moneychangers and declared His Father's house a place of prayer and not commerce. Derek decided to give his audience the night to ponder what they had learned, so he closed the session for the night.

In their room he and Sheila wondered about how many could speak English and understand what they had heard. Derek prayed it was not just his words, but the Holy Spirit that would talk to their hearts and make His will known to them. When they elected to take a walk in the late evening they felt accosted when Thom gave them a harsh warning. He said that they must remain inside because the night held much evil. They could see that he and several of the men had painted their faces white with blood-red T's extending across their foreheads and down their noses.

Derek felt defeated when they returned inside, wondering if God's message could find its way into the pagan hearts so long steeped in such rituals. Sheila had been more than a little frightened by the encounter and had urged him to secure the door. Although the same thought had crossed his mind, he was reminded of his own speech to her about trusting God for their security. Derek looked out the window and saw what looked like men patrolling the area and carrying machetes for defense against an unknown foe.

At dawn the village seemed to come alive with the sounds and smells of humanity. The couple awoke from their fitful sleep. A knock on their door was an invitation to breakfast in the great hall. They quickly washed in the cold water of the pitcher pump, dressed, and joined the smiling faces awaiting them. After a meal of corn cakes, honey, and cured spiced meat, Derek drew Thom aside.

"How many of the people can read and understand English?" he asked. "How many understand what I am saying?"

"Few can read, but most can understand English," Thom answered.

"How can that be? Derek asked. "If some don't know English, how can they understand what I say about Jesus?"

"They share with one another. We have known these stories since ancient times," Thom answered solemnly.

Derek was baffled. "How did this knowledge come to you?"

"The Great Spirit came, made these things known to us, and gave our fathers understanding of the things that you now teach."

"You knew these things before Pastor Brown and I came?"

"Yes, and before those who came before him," Thom said. "We have always known of the Father."

"Why do you allow us to come back and teach as though you were ignorant of these things?"

"There is much to learn. We learn it where we can. There is also much power in repeating the stories," Thom said quietly. "It helps the elders defeat the D-mans of the night."

Sheila interrupted their conversation to tell Derek that she was going to take a walk with the women of the village.

When Derek turned back to his host, he and the men of the tribe were gone. He found himself alone in the great hall.

As Derek walked about, he saw small gardens near each house. Scrawny plants propped up by small wooden fences were heavily laden with vegetables. He was amazed that they prospered, seemingly without nutrients and adequate water. Several ancient vehicles with rusting fenders and broken windows were scattered around the village, looking uncared for and deserted. *There is no visible source of fuel even if they could run*, he thought. But, remembering how they had used one of them to retrieve his Jeep, he assumed there was something that he could not see, perhaps an underground storage tank. Another anomaly caught his eye as he looked about. Above the door of each weathered structure was a series of red T's, each one looking freshly painted. He made a mental note to ask about their significance when he met with Thom again.

"Derek," Sheila called out, as she ran toward him. He turned at the sound of her voice. Her cheeks were rosy from the exercise, and she had a huge grin on her face. Following at her heels were a dozen small children laughing and smiling, and behind them were their mothers.

"Isn't it beautiful?" she asked him, indicating the valley surrounding them. "They have fruit trees."

Derek was surprised that his wife would find the desolate, arid desert beautiful, but humored her with a smile and said, "Yes, it is."

"What will you name him?" Thom asked, seeming to appear out of nowhere.

"Who?" Derek replied, wondering how the large man could move so swiftly and quietly.

"Your son," he replied, gesturing at Sheila.

"We haven't decided," Derek answered. It struck him for the first time that they might have a son, and he felt excited at the prospect.

While it had been light for over an hour, the sun was just peeking over the rocky cliffs of the surrounding mountains, and with it Derek began to see green trees and bushes dotting the landscape. He wondered how he had not noticed them when they entered the valley the previous day.

"Shall we hear more of the Jesus story?" Thom asked, while moving toward the meeting hall.

Derek followed, feeling misplaced and disillusioned. A small part of him was disappointed that the tribe wasn't totally dependent upon him for their spiritual education. He recognized the sin of pride that had taken hold of him - the feeling that it was he who brought salvation rather than simply being a tool of the Holy Spirit. He felt contrite as he began to speak, putting away notes and abandoning his script. He took the Bible in his hands and said, "Let's start at the beginning.

"In the beginning ..." As he read...they sat and returned his gaze with their eyes alive with anticipation. A few had their Bibles open and were following along. Most clutched them to their bosoms reverently, listening as he spoke. Thom and a few of the men occasionally nodded as they recognized a story. Some of the women whispered an explanation to the children from time to time.

Derek felt led to tell the "Jesus story" from Genesis through Revelation. He shared about a scarlet thread of redemption that ran through the entire Bible. He highlighted how God's grace can be found in each and every book of the Bible. After pointing them to the ram caught in the thicket on Mount Moriah from Genesis, the Passover lamb in Exodus, the Scapegoat set free in Leviticus, he stole a glance at his watch and was amazed at what the Holy Spirit was revealing to him on the fly. In each story he related how Jesus was represented in every story. These native people connected naturally to the stories involving sheep and goats. He went on to tell of the Bronze snake that would heal them if they only looked in faith as told in Numbers, and the manna that God brought on a daily basis in Deuteronomy. He went on to speak of the Commander of the Lord's army leading them into the Promised Land from the book of Joshua; the Angel of the Lord in Judges, and the Kinsman Redeemer in Ruth.

They broke for lunch, which gave Derek's vocal cords a rest. After lunch he continued on with the stories of King David and King

Solomon. Their eyes lit up when the stories of David were shared. They identified with David and his sling and Jonathan's arrows sent as a signal. They found it more difficult to connect to the riches of Solomon. He paused just long enough to take a sip of water, clear his throat, and return Sheila's smile. By the time they were ready to break for the evening meal, he had made it all the way to Psalms 22. It was the perfect picture of crucifixion given over a thousand years before Jesus went to the cross. *How was that possible?* Derek was amazed that even after hours of passionate teaching, he still seemed energized. He thanked God for the offered food and drink and sat down to enjoy the meal. He noticed there was a glow about Sheila, a vitality that he attributed to her pregnancy. It was odd that he hadn't really noticed it just days before.

"How am I doing?" he asked her casually.

"Wonderfully! I've never heard you share God's Word so clearly."

The fresh fruit and vegetables tasted delicious. He wondered how they kept them from spoiling in the heat and freezing in the cold. The meat appeared to be goat or sheep, which had been slowly cooked over an open flame. It too was a welcome treat. There was little talk or discussion during the meal. Derek found the mood around the table more subdued than at other times.

It was only a little after five with darkness quickly falling outside. When Thom indicated that everyone should go to their homes after the meal and return the next morning, Derek was surprised, but did not object. Although it still remained daylight outside, the sun had dropped behind the mountains. As the shadows replaced the sunlight, the mountains took on an ominous appearance. At their lodging, Derek

217

pointed out three newly painted red T's above the door.

"What do they mean?" Sheila asked as he closed the door.

"I am not sure," Derek answered. He then told her of his earlier discussion with Thom concerning the tribe's knowledge of Jesus.

They talked long into the night reliving events and sharing feelings. Before blowing out the candle at the bedside, Derek looked out the window and could clearly see one of the elders with a painted face swinging his machete in the darkness. His imagination caused him to think he also saw darker forms resembling wisps of smoke around the man. When he called Sheila to the window for a second opinion, the forms were gone.

To be continued.

Fissure II

During the night, troubling dreams filled Derek's mind. Terrifying images formed grotesque pictures on the canvas of his psyche before the light of dawn erased them. When Thom knocked on the door, Derek answered, invited him in, and began to ask him questions.

"What do the red markings above the doors mean?" he asked.

Thom was not quick to answer, but finally explained, "You read to us from Exodus where God sent the Angel of Death into Egypt, did you not?"

"I did," Derek answered, "Exodus chapter 11, verse 5."

"And did not God tell Moses to put the blood of the lamb on the door posts?"

"Yes, Exodus chapter 12, verse7." Derek replied, beginning to see the resemblance. "To protect the chosen ones from death."

"And are we not also the chosen of God who believe in the Savior?"

"We are."

"We use the cross to protect us from the D-mans of the night so that our families are safe inside while the elders fight and resist them outside," Thom explained.

It was clear to Derek that Thom meant demons, and the cross referred to the cross of crucifixion, which Christianity had adopted as a symbol of their faith. He was beginning to see how the primitive understanding, which had been handed down from one generation to another, had fostered those beliefs. He was, however, unwilling to believe in the necessity for such precaution in today's world.

"That was a one-time thing called down by God, Himself, against his enemies," he tried to explain. "As believers we are neither in jeopardy nor should we fear God's wrath."

"It is not God we fear," Thom said, shaking his head, "it is the D-mans of the Evil One."

Derek was neither prepared to discuss if demons existed, nor if they were a constant threat to the little village. "Have you seen the D-mans? Where do they come from?"

"Yes, many times. They come each night hoping to prey on the young and the unsaved. They live in the caves of our ancestors in the cliffs above."

"When did they first come?"

"Many generations ago when the Savior made Himself known to our ancestors, He threw them out while we still lived in the cliffs," he explained. "When we moved to the valley, they came back and brought others with them."

Derek recalled a passage of Scripture where a house was swept clean and the evil spirit was banished. Then later, it returned with others more evil than itself. Derek could see the parallel, but wondered if it wasn't simply an ancient legend.

"Why have your people not moved away?" he asked.

"Because God has blessed our valley, and we have learned that you cannot run away from evil," Thom answered. "Have you not noticed how the light has blessed the ground, how the trees and gardens prosper in His light?"

Derek could not deny that the water in the springs was sweet and cold, the fruit from the trees and vegetables from the gardens full of flavor and nutrients, all much out of character with the surrounding desert.

"We get a sprinkling of rain nearly every morning in the valley but not in the areas around us. Our soil grows crops when others do not," Thom said, trying to make his point.

Derek could find no rebuttal and remained silent.

"Shall we eat?" Thom asked, smiling.

Inside the hall, it was much as it had been before. The tribe was seated and waiting quietly. Tables were laden with fresh fruit (a form of Johnny cakes) and salt pork that had possibly come from a wild boar. Someone had mixed up some of the powdered milk which Derek and

Sheila had brought. It sat untouched until Sheila poured herself a glass and invited others to do the same. Once again Derek thanked God for the food. After the meal, Derek started reading in Proverbs and moved through Isaiah and Jeremiah. There was a murmur, a nodding of heads, and earnest looks among the assembled group as he described the beasts from Daniel's visions,. For the first time Derek was interrupted as he read.

Standing, Thom asked, "Are the things of which you read in the past or the future?"

"Of both. Daniel was seeing visions of things yet to come in his time. Some of those he was describing have already occurred, and others will occur at the end of days," he said, hoping that he could count on the Holy Spirit to edit and clarify for him.

Thom nodded, seemingly satisfied with the answer. They stopped for lunch, and the great hall was buzzing with conversation - some in English, but most in their native language. From the portion that Derek could understand, it was clear that the nature of the beasts from Daniel was being discussed.

After lunch Derek finished Daniel without further interruption and moved on through the Minor Prophets.

~ ~

As the world watched and waited, the countdown continued. Those sponsored from each nation included the brightest and most influential. Toward the end of the process, those with financial means purchased their way into the select group at staggering personal cost.

General Malloy had been chosen to assume ultimate command over the military and civilian contingents. The civilian group included scientific, operational and rich sightseers. The minimum operational crew was fifty per shift, or one hundred and fifty in total, with each working eight-hour shifts. A total of three hundred humans were being prepared to travel into space in just a few days.

Few in the entire world understood how particle transfer worked, or even knew for sure that it would work outside a lab. The process began with excited light waves and morphed into the decomposition of atoms borne by those waves. No one knew how the human body would be deconstructed, one atom at a time, then reconstructed at its destination, and what the possible long-term effect might be.

Christians were caught up in the frenzy as well, not taking time to consider if God was frowning or chuckling at mankind's puny attempt to discover where He had placed His throne. Several religious leaders, albeit not truly Christian ones, had secured space aboard with hopes of presenting themselves to God.

Every element on the chart was aboard the ship in varying quantities, ready to be used by the chemists to create and maintain everything they might need. Rather than store manufactured items, they would create them from raw materials during the voyage. A hologram would project the molecular structure of an item and computers would calculate the number of elements and process needed for reconstruction. The process was similar to that of reverse engineering. Computers contained the DNA of billions of known combinations, familiar and unfamiliar to everyday man, just waiting to be constructed as needed.

It stood nearly a quarter of a mile high, just over 1,200 feet, and

300 feet in diameter at its widest spot. No one knew its total cost, but it took the support of the entire world to construct and maintain. When it had flown initially, it used conventional and nuclear propulsion. This flight would use those as well, but only to escape gravity before resorting to the particle-projection transfer, and then again for maneuvering after arrival at various destinations. Twenty-eight hours, twelve minutes, fourteen seconds to lift off.

~ ~

"Have you ever gone to the caves during the daytime?" Derek asked Thom.

"No. To do so invites reprisal."

"Let me get this straight," Dexter said. "You believe that Jesus has chosen to bless you; that He continues to favor you and your village and provides for all of your needs; but yet you fear incurring the wrath of demons? Do you believe that the symbol of His cross has more power to protect than the Spirit of God living within you?"

Thom hung his head shamefully. "We lack faith," he admitted.

"Matthew chapter 28, verse 18 tells us who the Master is and who has dominion over the world. We read in First John chapter 4, verse 4, 'He who is in you is greater than he who is in the world.' Do you have mirrors in the village?" Derek asked. "If so, ask your people to bring them to the meeting hall."

Within a few minutes the men, women and even children arrived with all manner of mirrors, large and small, which they laid on the tables inside the hall.

"How many of the vehicles run and have headlights? Please move them between the houses facing toward the center."

Several of the men left after receiving instructions from Thom.

"Now please have wood brought here and placed in the center of the courtyard so that we may build a fire."

The sun was just dropping below the horizon when they returned, and the wood was piled high as instructed. Derek gathered the whole tribe inside the hall and spoke to them with conviction, holding his Bible high above his head. Thom translated his words with the same fierce tone in his voice.

"We will call on the name of Jesus, the Light of the World, to dispel the darkness and overcome the D-mans. Stand in front of your homes, hold your Bibles high, face the darkness you fear, and repeat God's Word after me. Hold the mirrors in front of you as a symbol of your faith in Jesus, and let the light shine from Him and through you. None will need to paint their faces or carry machetes. Jesus will fight for you and overcome your enemies."

The crowd looked at one another with concern and then back at Derek and Thom.

Thom nodded his head in agreement and smiled. "Jesus is Lord," he said.

Outside, Derek bent and lighted the kindling under the wood. As it began to grow, the fingers of flame cast eerie shadows on the surrounding structures. The villagers stood at the doors of their homes, ready to retreat inside while watching the fire increase in size. When the lights of the cars came to life, both hope and fear were written plainly across their faces. At his side, Sheila was holding the mirror from her

225

purse and her worn Bible. The light of the fire reflected in her eyes. Derek held his Bible in one hand and a visor from the Jeep in the other. The mirror faced the raging fire.

Time seemed to stand still. They came from the darkness like wisps of dirty, black smoke. Their features were contorted and changing. Their evil, red eyes shined as they danced around the fire, curiously watching the assembled villagers.

Derek focused the beam of light from his mirror toward the dancing figures and quoted Scripture, "Jesus is the Light of the World. The light shines in the darkness and the darkness does not overpower it. He who is in me is greater than he who is in the world."

He waited as the Pueblos followed his lead, and then repeated himself. "Let the light of Jesus shine in the darkness and lead us into the light," he said, stepping forward toward the fire.

Noises, unearthly and frightening, filled the night.

Derek was making it up as he went now, quoting every verse he could think of concerning light and calling on Jesus to overcome the enemy.

The many dancing figures of smoke were merging now, congealing into one, becoming less transparent, and growing in size until forty red eyes were staring from a single head that towered ten feet above them.

"He who is in me …," Derek began again.

"Ye of little faith," the voice boomed out of the darkness, quoting Jesus' words. "How can you call on the One who you do not know? You speak of things you do not believe."

Derek held his Bible high above his head. "You have been

defeated by the blood of the Lamb and the word of our testimony. We who believe in His strength and power renounce you in the name of Jesus. You have neither power over us nor any permission to harass us. Our sins have been forgiven and Jesus reigns in our lives."

There was a single shriek as the smoke from the towering figure was consumed and rose upward with the smoke of the fire. All was quiet.

~ ~

Sixteen hours, fifteen minutes, and ten seconds to the launch. Like iron shavings to a magnet, they came from all over the world. Thoughts, almost tangible in their substance, were drawn to the great looming masterpiece that was built by mankind to challenge the very existence of God. Like wisps of fog finding entrance into the body of the great beast through the fissure, thoughts of lust, greed, deceit, immoral and unclean acts, covetousness, lies, slander, gossip, inflicting pain and injury, conquest and humiliation, retribution and death found their way through the impenetrable hull of the great ship.

The similarity of the world's focus of the building and launch of the towering space vehicle to that of the Tower of Babel did not go unnoticed by the Christian leaders of the world. Those who were caught up in the frenzy dismissed their warnings as foolishness. Once launched and tested, there was no plan to return it to Earth. They would leave it in orbit, and use shuttles to and from Earth to resupply as needed after it had completed the assigned stellar explorations. In many ways the undertaking mirrored the fictional events depicted in the *Star Trek* television show of the late 1900s.

227

Over the past several years, the total accumulated knowledge of the world doubled and redoubled itself at an alarming rate, making mankind almost incidental to the electronic machinery it had created. While nations had retained their names and some degree of autonomy, more realistically the world was led by a small group of individuals. They had taxing and enforcement powers granted them by the reconstructed United Nations of which membership was mandatory. Indisputably, Arthros ruled the world with an iron hand; the ten members of the Security Council were just his puppets. Had they chosen otherwise, they would have likely just disappeared and been replaced.

~ ~

The dawning of the day brought with it not only the resplendence of its welcomed light and early morning rain, but a recommitment of the entire tribe to their Savior. The dying embers of last night's fire were quenched by the raindrops, never to be needed again. Its ashes were spread over the gardens to provide nutrition to the soil. Of the Pueblos, the Hopi and several others had long known of Jesus and His saving grace, but only this small band had seen it up close and personal. Derek took all day to share the "Jesus story" from the New Testament.

They seemed enlivened when the words turned red in the text, as though they could hear their Master speaking. Derek was enjoying sharing the gospel story in this unique place and culture. Each word passed his lips with an unusual reverence and sweetness, and was delivered with clarity and conviction to his listening audience. It was still early afternoon when he finished reading Jude's prayer.

"This last book of our Bible speaks of things yet to come; things that will be done to complete the plan the Father has for His creation. No man fully understands the mind of God. They are called mysteries because many things about God are beyond our understanding."

He could hear his words being repeated and translated to others in the room.

His preface, he hoped, would reduce the number of unanswerable questions that always seemed to accompany a study of The Revelation. He hoped to establish himself as learned, but humble, and not all knowing. He read the few pages introducing and explaining the book, which the translators had included for clarification.

The apostle John, the Holy Spirit, and His servant Derek combined their considerable resources to paint pictures in the minds of the audience that would have made the director of the epic Ten Commandments green with envy. Each character and event came alive, and was woven into the fabric of the story to open the minds, hearts and eyes of those present, including Pastor Derek.

The large hall grew quiet as he read John's final warning, "I testify to everyone who hears the words of the prophecy of this book. If anyone adds to them, God will add to him the plagues which are written in this book; and if anyone takes away from the words of the book of this prophecy, God will take away his part from the tree of life and from the holy city, which are written in this book. He who testifies to these things says, "Yes, I am coming quickly." Amen. Come, Lord Jesus. The grace of the Lord Jesus be with all. Amen."

Derek and Sheila felt refreshed and strengthened in their faith, eager to face other challenges and share their witness. At the same time, they were saddened to be leaving their new friends. Thom approached them with his tribe gathered behind. All were grinning broadly.

"Friends," he said, "by your faith you have given us strength and renewed our faith as well. Thank you."

Derek was still thinking of an appropriate response when Sheila said, "We have chosen a name for our son," she said. "We will name him Thomas, but call him Tom."

Her words elicited a quick response as Thom repeated her words to the tribe proudly.

As they began their journey back home, they stopped at the junction of the three dirt roads. Derek got out of the Jeep, and with all the symbolism he could muster he searched and found a fitting stone. He placed it on end as a permanent monument that marked the road to the village and named the place El Shaddai, God Almighty.

~ ~

As the time for launch neared, thousands of reporters and teams of video staff were becoming more and more anxious to scoop each other in what they viewed as the biggest event since creation. With little news to report, tempers grew short as tension continued to build, resulting in many fights and several shootings. The impromptu city that sported makeshift casinos, brothels and bars encouraged illegal activities, such as drug trade and theft. Profiteers were selling water for twenty-five dollars a gallon, and likewise bread by the loaf. Gasoline to run generators was metered out by the liter. There was madness about the whole macabre event, causing people to quit their jobs and sell or mortgage their homes just to attend.

Arthros and his ilk lived in decadent luxury in a palace-like structure built just for the occasion, having their every worldly craving and desire catered to as they awaited the event. The fissure was drawing more and more darkness from them, and finally could not hold one more depraved or impure thought. The fissure sealed itself and disappeared.

Finally the great ship was loaded with its many passengers, beginning with security and operations personnel, housekeeping and food preparation, scientific types, and sightseeing passengers. Every passenger wore a sending and receiving headset that transmitted their speech to a computer, where it was analyzed and rebroadcast in the preselected languages for anyone within a fifty-mile radius. With over two hundred nations working closely together, communications was a must.

A final inspection of the ship's exterior showed no flaws. Inside, its systems reported operating at one hundred percent efficiency. The doors were sealed and the clock began to count down the final minutes. Giant stadiums worldwide sold tickets to the hundreds of millions who desired to witness the event and live it vicariously through the passengers on board. It became the ultimate reality show. Interactive bios of the travelers were available for sale to their fans on Earth, with downloads and updates going directly to personal phones and computers. True believers worldwide fell to their knees, bowed their heads, and asked forgiveness as man prepared to challenge God's transcendence.

~ ~

Derek's church members had been inside the sanctuary for only twenty minutes praying for God's grace and mercy when they received word of the launch. Minutes passed slowly before news of the ship breaking free of the Earth's gravity was released to the waiting world. The ship's crew had just enabled the ship's computer to begin the progression that took them from conventional propulsion to light speed. All at once the communication's internal computer failed. It stopped without warning, leaving the crew with only conventional voice communication. Immediately there were 150 languages and dialects talking at once. Next the darkness seemed to seep from the pores of the ship's interior into their hearts, filling each with evil, darkness and despair. They began to argue and fight, plot and scheme against each other. They took up weapons and attacked one another in their rage. The nose of the ship set a new course, away from the blackness of space and into the waiting arms of the sun. Everyone on Earth held their breath in horror, watching the pandemonium take place via cameras.

Suddenly there was darkness. The sun's light stopped. The moon had nothing to reflect and the stars disappeared into the blackness. Men and women screamed in terror. Generated light was so feeble in the darkness that it was totally consumed. Seconds went by as the great ship hurdled toward the blackened sun at light speed, finally striking its molten mass. Upon impact the light of God's presence devoured the darkness like a hungry wolf, consuming the night and the vanity of man. Jesus, the Light of the World, appeared everywhere at once. Every eye saw and every knee bowed before the King of Kings.

Of Places and Things

She had read every book in the house, pouring over them from cover to cover, voraciously devouring page after page. The subject matter did not seem to matter much, although her personal choice would have been of remote and faraway places where her own imagination could paint pictures in her mind.

Mousy, a single word that most aptly described the gangly thirteen year old whose mind raced to keep up with her body. She was what many called at that awkward stage between being a child and an adult, or pre-puberty. Her arms and legs made her body seem long and angular, her breasts were underdeveloped, and her nose was too prominent for her small features. Her one redeeming feature was her long, beautiful hair, which showcased her face still unblemished by acne. As a result of her Irish heritage, freckles adorned her pale nose, cheeks, and bony shoulders.

Thankfully, she seemed not to care a great deal about the tastes of others. Had she been concerned about fashion, her parents' "off the rack" budget would have produced a nightmare of contradictions of both color and style. She was not unaware of fashion trends, but was less concerned about it than others her age. At school she came and went, mostly without notice, and her appointed chair was either filled or empty at particular dates and times. "Speak when spoken to" was the mantra of her father and mother. It was a phrase handed down from generations of adults who were yet to value the minds and opinions of the young people growing up in their house.

From earliest memory Amanda had stayed out of conversations, fearful of saying the wrong words or showing her ignorance of the subject at hand. She was a shadow on the periphery of the picture. The focal point at any gathering was always the more sociable and extroverted children. From the beginning her parents called her Manda, which seemed to express how they had shortchanged her by not even making the effort to include all the letters of her name when they spoke it. Her eyes, clear and intelligent, could not quite decide what color they wanted to be: gray, blue or hazel.

Father, as she always referred to him, was the dean at the local state college, a man whose position, if not his personality, demanded respect. Introverted, scholarly and a stickler for detail, he controlled the small institution by a myriad of policies and regulations most of which he had personally instituted. Their home was much the same with notes and lists posted on appliances, mirrors, and at appropriate places throughout the house to remind, correct, and prevent his family from abridging the rules.

He was frugal, not out of necessity, but because of his need to control conditions and situations around him, and in that to control others under his tutelage. He would turn off their old car at a light if it appeared the wait might be longer than he deemed necessary. He would depress the clutch on downhill slopes and coast toward a stop sign from half a block away to save wear and tear on the brake linings. His wife, Nellie, had been subject to his rule since age seventeen when they married, and now at forty could not imagine a world without his special brand of order.

Amanda was an only child because it seemed prudent to raise only those one could easily care for and support. It was a matter of fiscal responsibility that many did not feel. Her father often reminded his small family about this when he saw the smiling faces of a half dozen children in hand-me-down clothes. Amanda secretly longed for a brother or sister, and when she was younger often invented one with which to play. But now, the books provided her escape with heroes, friends and siblings. When she first read *Peter Pan* she had been Wendy, and later became Nancy Drew. Exotic places and people of legend and history provided the adventure her soul required.

Amanda was almost fourteen when an aneurism burst in her mother's brain, causing her to go into a coma and later to die. Her father took the loss in stride, expecting that Amanda would fill her mother's shoes. During her first year of high school the demands of cooking, cleaning and laundry caused her grades to drop from a perfect 4.0 to a 3.8, enraging her father beyond reason.

They were called "witnesses" by outsiders, both Christians and non-believers. Others who categorized them with Mormons and less mainstream faiths called their group a sect. Knowing little else, the faith seemed real and fulfilling to her as a child, but less so as she read and reread the Holy Bible from cover to cover. The Holy Spirit was at work in her, bringing questions to mind, challenging her faith time and again,

235

and leading her toward the salvation Jesus offered to those who followed Him. But there was no place to go and no one to talk to concerning spiritual things - certainly not her rigid and unyielding father. At the school library, and later the public library, she would devour book after book of Bible commentary in her search for truth.

During her junior year her body began to develop and blossom into womanhood, causing her father to enforce a strict dress code to hide it from the sinful world. Her year-round wardrobe consisted of long skirts, dresses, and long-sleeved garments that were unflattering and bulky. The summer she turned sixteen she began to see the looks her father had been giving her that showed more than a fatherly interest. She began to lock her bedroom door at night. On more than one occasion she heard footsteps in the hall and the lock being tested before the footsteps receded. Boys at school had also noticed the shy girl with long hair who kept to herself. On several occasions she had been asked on a date, only to be forced to refuse by her father.

As a senior and an honor student, she was allowed certain freedoms at school, one of which was to travel with the debate team. For the first time in her life she spent a night away from home. Although her father disliked the idea, he was forced to embrace it as part of her necessary academic development. As co-captain of the team, Amanda received personal recognition when the team won time after time, ultimately finding themselves in the state competition. Her vast book knowledge made her a formidable opponent, and her concise speech left little room for misinterpretation when she made a point or offered rebuttal. The environment allowed her to see and taste, for the first time, some of the world she had heretofore only read about. When she returned home, her father tried to put the butterfly back in its cocoon, only to find it was now impossible. Graduating cum laude, Amanda was surprised to find she had garnered many friends and well-wishers during her high school years, simply because of her desire to avoid social politics. Her unwillingness to share or listen to gossip prevented most from having a reason to call her neutrality into question. Later when she was offered a full scholarship at a small university in Virginia, her father could neither dissuade her nor break her resolve to go.

~ ~

While she had little idea of what she wanted in life, she knew what she did not want. She did not want the bland, unrewarding life her mother had lived. Because of the university's proximity to the nation's capital, many of her peers were political science majors with dreams to someday hold office or work in government. Similarly, Amanda had been recruited because of her prowess on the debate team and the potential of being a competent politician. After much deliberation and discussion, she focused on the Foreign Service aspect of government and saw herself working in an embassy in some exotic land. Having excelled in high school French, she added two new foreign languages to her studies at the university and audited a French class.

While her scholarship provided for her basic housing and food requirements, it did not offer the extras needed to enjoy her newfound freedom. Her father sent her a monthly stipend sufficient for bus tokens and personal hygiene, but little else. However, in His wisdom, God opened doors to her as a tutor for those struggling with French. That allowed her to make friends, integrate into the college life, and earn an income. At midterm both her attendance and grades were perfect. She had made several friends, and they would often go see the many sights in and around Washington, DC. When her father called and offered her a train ticket home over the holidays, she gracefully declined, saying she needed the extra time to study.

She was nineteen when she went on her first date. It was only lunch at an off campus coffee shop with a young man from her French class. Jasper Duncan, also a freshman, was from the West Coast. His family lived in a small town in the liberal-leaning state of Oregon. Because of the cost of airfare and the uncertainty of travel in midwinter, he also elected to remain at school during Christmas vacation. Jasper was self-confident, yet shy and self-deprecating. A little over six feet with sun-bleached, light brown hair and a quick smile, he was a devout Christian. When he asked her to accompany him to church the following Sunday she accepted with anticipation and reservations based upon her upbringing.

It felt like a long awaited homecoming when she entered the building. Fear and trepidation fell away as the pastor went right to the Bible for his sermon, and then used it time and again to support his points. She was stirred when the offer came to go forward and accept Jesus, but forced herself to ignore the invitation. Jasper assumed she was already a Christian, and therefore did not find it necessary to ask.

"How long have you been coming here?" Amanda asked.

"About four months," Jasper answered. "Ever since I got settled in. Where do you go?"

"I haven't," she admitted truthfully, "but I like it here."

He smiled. "Maybe you'd like to join me on Wednesday nights for Bible study."

Amanda hesitated, wondering if she was moving too fast. "I'll give it a try, but no long-term commitment. OK?"

"Fair enough," he answered. "But I know you'll get hooked, just like I did."

They continued to see each other during the break, spending Sundays together at church and Wednesday evenings in young adult Bible study. Amanda wanted to ask questions about Jesus but hesitated, knowing that most if not all were already believers and would know what she was ashamed to ask. Each Sunday her embarrassment made her ignore God's calling when the invitation came. She began to convince herself that she was living a lie and considered going to another church. Her heart told her that the same would happen there - that she was running from salvation in order to avoid being exposed as a non-believer.

School resumed and life returned to normal. As she was reading her Bible alone in the dorm one day, two Scriptures jumped from the pages: Matthew chapter 6, verse 24, "No one can serve two masters; for either he will hate the one and love the other, or he will be devoted to one and despise the other. You cannot serve God and wealth." And Matthew chapter 10, verse 33, "But whoever denies Me before men, I will also deny Him before My Father who is in heaven." Tearfully and humbly she prayed for forgiveness and asked Jesus to come into her life, accepting Him as her Lord and Savior. She then called Jasper. When he answered, she was still crying, but at the same time jubilant. She apologized to him for not setting the record straight from the beginning. He was very happy for her. He had nothing to say about her reluctance to admit her need; he simply desired to share in her happiness.

The second half of the year seemed to go by quickly. Before she knew it the cherry trees were in bloom and finals were staring them in the face. She was reluctant to return home and face her father, knowing that he would never accept her newfound joy. His doctrine was so deeply ingrained and he was so inflexible and closed to discussion, she saw it as a potential breaking point in their relationship. She avoided the subject until she could no longer evade it, and told him that she was going to remain and take summer classes. He did not offer much resistance, but promised to try and visit when he was able.

Amanda did well in Spanish and Russian and was able to pursue another semester of each during the summer. She added a couple of electives in world history and geography, fourteen credits in all. She was able to stay on campus and work in the library. Jasper, however, was eager to return to his family in Bend, Oregon, and take time to relax and forget about school. She was able to pick up two other students to tutor, and had banked several hundred dollars by summer's end.

~ ~

While they had talked several times by phone, she and Jasper allowed other priorities dominate their summer. When he arrived a week before the fall semester began he had a surprise for her. He rented a car and invited her to join him on a trip up the coast. She was torn between wanting to enjoy the trip and his companionship, and worrying about them being young, single and traveling alone. She delayed giving him her answer and prayed for God's guidance. Her prayers were answered when he also invited two other girls in their Bible study class to join them. The four got as far as southern Maine before being forced to return for the start of the fall term. She had a wonderful time and enjoyed her friends and a freedom she had never known. She saw places, sights and new things she had only read about in books, never believing she would ever experience them herself. When they arrived back on campus her father was waiting for her.

He had arrived unannounced two days before and was in no mood to hear her explanations or excuses. When she made the mistake of telling him that her two Christian girl friends had served as chaperones, he looked at them with distain and called them Jezebels before calling a cab and leaving. That was the last time she spoke to him, and the last time she saw her father alive.

The semester began on a low note for her with the memory of the look in her father's eyes haunting her, and Satan using the event to try and cause her to doubt her faith. When she rejected Jasper's efforts to speak with her and did not return his calls, he stopped by the library where she worked, handed her a sealed envelope, and left without speaking.

The note said: Do you have dreams? What would a perfect life look like to you if you could choose one? If you were granted only one wish what would it be? Would you live your life over if you could? How would you change it? Who is the most important person in your life? What do you want to leave behind when you die? What would you like to hear others saying about you if you listened in at your own funeral? What is the purpose of your life … of any life? Can we have lunch together tomorrow? Jasper

Amanda was a deep thinker by nature who had only lately developed a sense of humor. When she came to the last question she couldn't resist smiling. *It wasn't his fault,* she thought to herself. *It is mine for not being honest with my father in the first place. I should have called and told him I was leaving for a short trip with friends. And whether he approved or not, at least he wouldn't have wasted a trip.*

She called Jasper and said, "Yes, I'd love to have lunch with you. As for the rest of the questions, I'll have to think them over."

"See you tomorrow then," he replied.

Amanda spent the night considering what Jasper had written, and stayed up late to try and answer each question honestly.

Jasper was waiting when she arrived at the little bistro on campus. He smiled as she walked up. "I hope you are hungry."

"Starved," she replied, sitting next to him at the small table. "I've been looking forward to this all morning."

Jasper was still smiling when Amanda pulled some papers from her backpack.

"You know you kept me up half of the night, don't you?" she said accusingly but with a coy smirk on her face.

While they waited for their lunch, she began to answer the questions he had left with her.

"Dreams? Yes, I do have dreams. But not specific ones like most people. I dream of seeing many of the things I have only read about in books. Perfect life? I am not sure I can honestly answer number two. I have never known anyone with a perfect life. One wish? For happiness for me and those I love, but I won't know what that is until I have lived it. Live your life over? No, once is enough. But I'd change the way I handled things last week with my father if I could. Most important person? Jesus, no question, but you are important too," she said with a grin. "Leave behind when you die? It sounds corny when you say it out loud. I just want the world to be a better place than it was when I came."

He nodded and smiled when she stopped and took a long drink of her iced tea.

"My funeral? I haven't given much thought as to what kind of legacy I'd like to leave behind," she said. "It'd be nice to hear that I made a difference in someone's life, and that something I said or did actually helped someone or made their life better. I researched the last one in the Bible," she said. "We were all created to bring God praise and glory." She stopped talking, leaned toward him, and folded her hands waiting for his reply.

Finally, after several minutes Jasper asked, "Where are we going?"

She feigned ignorance. "Back to class after we finish eating," she said with a smile.

He gave her a very serious look and said, "I mean is there an us? Can you see the possibility that we could become more than friends?"

Amanda's heart raced as she considered how she wanted to answer. "The short answer is yes, but it is complicated for me," she answered gently. "Can we get together tonight after French class?"

She couldn't tell if he was pleased or disappointed by what she had said.

"I need to study for tomorrow's test. Can we talk and study together?"

"Library at six?" she asked.

"It's a date."

~ ~

She had back-to-back classes followed by an hour break before French class. She went to the library to conjugate German verbs and do a little memory work. As she sat in the quiet of the library her mind was too cluttered to concentrate on German. She ran Jasper's question over and over in her mind. *Is there an us?* Amanda was new to prayer and not quite comfortable yet with just how to approach God. *Father, You are the only One who really knows me, how I feel and what I am feeling now about Jasper. Help me, help us to make good decisions and do whatever pleases You. I want to please You. Amen.* She didn't know exactly what she expected, but the lack of divine inspiration left her wanting more.

She arrived early to class and took a few minutes to visit with those she tutored and set up times for their next meeting. One of the girls looked up and smiled at Jasper when he came in. This caused Amanda to feel a little twinge of jealousy. She purposely excused herself, sat beside him, and struck up a conversation. She knew that what she had done was "high school", but couldn't seem to stop herself. When the prof called the session to order, talking stopped and the focus was on him and his white board. He usually gave the full lesson in French, but today he bounced back and forth forcing his students to adapt without thinking as he integrated both languages together.

Amanda followed along without difficulty, picturing herself in Paris strolling through the marketplace or some of the shops, haggling over prices, asking directions, ordering meals, and seeing the sights. In

her imagination she was living the dream that Jasper had asked about
earlier. They broke into groups, half with scripted dialogue and the other
half asked to respond without aid. Halfway through the exercise they
changed roles.

When she and Jasper arrived at the library she was still unclear
of what she truly felt and what she should say. He sat quietly across from
her at the table with an expectant look on his face.

"Jasper, we have really never talked much about ourselves and
our lives when we were growing up."

She told him of her family life: her lack of interaction with
outsiders, (those outside of the witness church), her lack of social life,
and finally her inexperience with the opposite sex. She also explained
how she lived life through books, and of her first visit away from home
with the debate team. He listened quietly, said nothing, and nodded
occasionally.

"I almost feel like a butterfly coming out of a cocoon.
Everything is new to me, overwhelming, exciting, and also a bit
frightening," she said.

He still had not spoken, but she could see compassion in his
eyes.

"I have feelings for you, but I am not sure what they are or even
what they are supposed to be," she said.

"I am sorry for pushing you. I had no idea," he said. "I care
about you and wanted to make that clear. I also wanted to see if I am
wasting my time, or if you feel the same about me."

Her eyes were rimmed with tears as she took his hand. "I do
care. I have never felt this way about anyone before, but I don't know if

it is enough for a lifetime commitment."

He smiled, and then laughed gently. "I just wanted to know if you liked me. I didn't ask you to marry me."

"Can we just be friends for a while and see where God leads us?"

Jasper nodded and smiled. "So is it too early in our friendship to ask you to fly home with me at Christmas and meet the family?" he asked jokingly.

"Could it be worse than you meeting my father?"

"That'll be for you to decide, if we go. They're good folks, but you may find them a bit overwhelming compared with where you are coming from."

~ ~

She attempted to call her father to apologize and explain herself to him, but he didn't answer. After several attempts she gave up trying.

Jasper took a part-time job in a local bike shop, working a few hours a week, while Amanda continued to tutor and work at the library. She gradually replaced the teaching of the witnesses with the truth of God's Word concerning Jesus and salvation. On December 15 she was called into the dean's office and received word that her father had died. She was forced to use her meager savings to fly home to make the funeral arrangements. When she arrived she found that his church had been bequeathed all of his assets. The church had also made arrangements for his burial without contacting her. She took a few belongings of her own and several of her mother's keepsakes, and then returned to school broke, lost and alone.

Pain and bitterness followed her wherever she went. Her usual sunny disposition was buried with her father. Jasper rejected his family's offer to go home for Christmas, electing to stay and lend his support to her. Their pastor met with them several times, attempting to help her learn to forgive and accept God's comfort.

When school resumed in January, Amanda had officially achieved junior status as a result of her summer classes. She was excited when she received two written inquiries concerning her plans following graduation. One inquiry was from the State Department and the other from a private enterprise interested in her for her language skills. Both sent representatives to meet with her, and while they did not make offers of employment, they made suggestions of several other languages she might consider adding to her growing list.

~ ~

When plane tickets for Jasper and Amanda arrived from his parents, her first thought was to graciously refuse their generosity. A single line from a Bible study friend haunted her as she considered it. "To reject the gift is to reject the giver." Of course the context had been that one who rejects Jesus' gift of salvation was also rejecting Jesus. In the end they caught a plane headed west for the two weeks of spring break with time to relax and try to forget about school. When their flight landed in Portland, Oregon, they found their connection on a small, commuter plane that took them to Salem. They were met at the airport by Jasper's family. Jasper's father was tall with a military bearing. His mother, a strawberry blond, was only five feet tall, with a ready smile and a twinkle in her green eyes. Jasper's brother Lou, sister Connie, sister-in-law, and young nephew rounded out the welcoming party. Since they had arrived early in the day, the family planned to show their guest around the state capital before driving home to Bend.

Amanda immediately felt welcomed and accepted, but felt like a pauper when she clutched her purse knowing that the $150 inside was all the money she had in the world. Dane, Jasper's dad, declined her offer to pay her way at lunch saying simply, "You are our guest. Save your money in case you want to buy souvenirs."

Lou's wife and Connie went out of their way to make sure Amanda felt comfortable and included wherever they went. Apparently they had an itinerary already planned that included lots of junk food, points of interest, and several of the shops in the outlet mall in Woodburn. By late afternoon they were in the forested mountains that separated the two towns. Amanda marveled at how green everything seemed with the white of the winter's snow as a backdrop.

"Have you ever skied?" Connie asked.

"No, I've never spent much time in the out of doors."

"We'll fix that," Jasper's mother said with a smile. "Dad's got Jasper's snowmobile ready to go and we have plenty of warm gear to go around."

When she looked over at Jasper, he winked at her without speaking. Everything seemed oversized to Amanda, distances farther, trees taller, even modest houses on estate sized lots, and an outgoing friendly way about the people that encouraged them to interact with each other. Rustic maybe, but not rundown or unkempt, the family house had the look of a comfortable cabin. The snow had been plowed, leaving the driveway clear. An old Dodge Power Wagon, with a hydraulic blade, stood ready to repeat the task when needed. Amanda had never driven nor needed to. Until now, that had seemed quite normal to her. It looked like everyone on this side of the Rockies had their own vehicle. Public transportation was nearly non-existent. When they pulled to a stop, Jasper was excited to show her his prize, a 1976 Ford F250 four-wheel drive. Even before they took their luggage inside she was given the privilege of sitting in the White Goose and listening to its throaty pipes as he started it up for her. She could see the little boy who still existed in him as he pointed out its many custom features and promised her a ride.

The house was very spacious, with large rooms and a second story behind the great room that faced outward toward the driveway. Cedar, she was told, was the choice of the local builders. It is a soft wood, but at home in the moist climate of the Pacific Northwest. It gave the home a rough-hewn, masculine look that spoke of durability and utility rather than fashion. Only the bedrooms and baths were sheet rocked and painted. The remainder of the house had stained wood. A large, rock fireplace lined one wall of the living room and appeared to be a central gathering place for family and guests alike.

"You can bunk with me," Connie offered, directing Amanda to her bedroom. "Excuse the mess. I just got in yesterday and haven't taken time to pick up."

It was obviously a girl's room, but not in a typical feminine way. There were no pink curtains or dolls left over from grade school, and no prom pictures or romance novels on the shelves. Amanda was intrigued at this young woman who seemed self-confident and independent.

"What's your major?" Amanda asked, as she hung her clothes in the closet.

"Marine biology. If we get a chance, I'll take you over to Newport and show you around."

"Thank you. I'd like that."

"How about you?" Connie asked. "Whatcha gonna be when you grow up?"

Amanda laughed. "Languages, foreign languages. I hope they will be my ticket to see the world someday."

"Chili's ready," came the call from downstairs where the rest of the family had already gathered around a long, wooden table.

Amanda noticed that there was an open chair beside Jasper. After the blessing was asked upon the food, the family jumped right to the business at hand without further invitation or ceremony. They caught up on each other's lives as they ate, firing questions at Jasper and Amanda between bites of food. Amanda learned that Lou and Nancy lived a few miles away. He worked at the local auto parts store, and Nancy taught school. Jasper's dad owned and ran a logging business. Jasper's mom, Donna, was content to volunteer at the church, keep house, and watch her grandson. To Amanda it was almost too much information too soon. Her brain was overloaded with the newness of the surroundings and this robust lifestyle.

"If you'll hold Glen, Mom and I'll clean up the dishes," Nancy said, handing her son to Amanda.

Amanda had never held a child before, but she was given no opportunity to refuse. She and little Glen, who was squirming to get away, joined Connie and the men beside the fireplace. Jasper smiled but said nothing as she sat down.

"Jasper tells us that you want to do something in the Foreign Service or diplomatic corps, and that you've already been recruited some," Dane said.

She was caught a little off guard. "That seems to be the direction that things are moving, but it is all so new to me that I'm still not sure."

"How about CIA?" Connie asked with a chuckle. "Given that any thought?"

When they all laughed, she laughed along, but secretly wondered if it may be another option. When the other two women joined them, Lou asked, "Anyone up for a moonlight ride before bedtime? The snowcats are gassed and ready to go."

Jasper looked hopeful but held back, waiting for Amanda to answer.

"It's two o'clock in the morning on the East Coast. These two have been traveling all day. I'll bet they'd enjoy it more after they have had some rest," Donna said.

Amanda felt relieved while she guessed that Jasper was a little disappointed.

"Tomorrow then," Dane said. "It might be better to go in the daylight for her first ride." He winked at Amanda. "Tomorrow's Saturday, so we can take our time and have a nice run."

~ ~

When Amanda awoke, she expected to see the familiar surroundings of her small dorm room. Instead, Connie's empty bed and the smell of frying bacon greeted her. The clock by the bedside read eight o'clock, but she quickly converted that to eleven Eastern time and felt guilty for sleeping so late. She quickly brushed her teeth, washed her face, and put on fresh clothes before going into the kitchen to join Jasper's family.

Jasper smiled when he saw her. "Just in time. Breakfast is about ready. Lou and Nancy are not here yet."

Donna had just taken a huge stack of bacon from the frying pan and started the eggs.

"Can I help?" Amanda asked, seeing the family watching her.

Donna smiled. "You can watch the spuds, and turn them when they're ready if you like."

Amanda saw a large, cast iron skillet full of hash browned potatoes, onions and bell peppers on the stove.

Dane went to stoke the fire and add some wood. Jasper and Connie began to set the table and pour juice.

Seeing the helpless look on Amanda's face, Donna said to Amanda quietly, "Peek under them with a spatula and wait until they are good and brown before you turn them. They'll be nice and crispy that way."

Amanda smiled her thanks.

As Lou, Nancy and little Glenn arrived, the eggs, hash browns and bacon were put on the table.

After breakfast, the men hurriedly dressed and went out to start the machines while the women stacked the dishes in the sink and slipped into their snowsuits. Amanda tried on the suit that Connie wore in high school. It fit her quite well, and with the addition of boots, gloves and a helmet, she was ready to go. With four machines and seven riders, plus Glen, they doubled up. Nancy rode behind Lou and had Glen in a papoose pack that hung between them. Dane and Donna shared the big sled. Amanda rode with Jasper, and Connie was on her own. They took the trail that began behind the house and wound twenty miles to the top of the mountain.

The fresh, crisp air put color on their cheeks. They enjoyed brief rests with hot chocolate and coffee. For the first time, Amanda had her arms around Jasper. It felt good, natural and reassuring to hold herself against him. He taught her to lean into the curves and use her legs for balance. The twenty miles went by quickly.

They soon found themselves on the summit looking down on the white expanse of the valley floor. Jasper pointed out landmarks and points of interest, throwing in humorous stories about his childhood. As he spoke, Amanda wondered if it was necessary to travel abroad to find her dreams. Maybe they were right here before her, awaiting her response.

YOU MIGHT ALSO BE INTERESTED IN...

Heaven Help Us

Short Stories Volume One

AND

Available in print form and Apple &

Android applications Find them at

www.prayerfulpublishing.com

Made in the USA
Lexington, KY
10 November 2019